D1282749

New Shanghai Cuisine

New Shanghai Cuisine
Bridging the old and the new

Jereme Leung

Marshall Cavendish
Cuisine

Dedication

For my mother, Kwong Wai Chan.
Her courage, love and encouragement
have always been my source of inspiration.

appetisers & cold dishes

soups

seafood

poultry

meat

vegetables & bean curd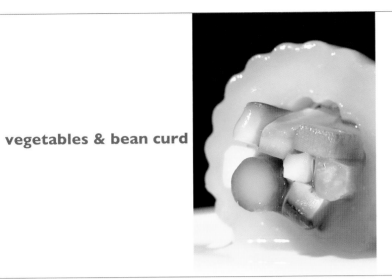

 **rice & noodles**

 dim sum

desserts

Contents

I would like to thank the following individuals and establishments
for giving me tremendous support and help
in putting together this book.

Acknowledgements

For making this book possible, I would like to thank David Yip, Violet Phoon, Jamilah Mohd Hassan, Lydia Leong, Lynn Chin, and the entire team at Marshall Cavendish International (Asia) for making an idea a reality.

I am grateful for the support and encouragement from the investors and management team of Three on the Bund. Thanks to Mr. and Mrs. Liem, our Chairman Cherie Liem and Co-Chairman Handel Lee. Special thanks also to Patrick Yeoh, Richard Helfer, Paul Liu, Alan Hepburn and Dagmar Lyons for supporting my ideas and beliefs.

Thanks to Choon, the CEO and founder of Simplylife Group, and Grace Liu of Asianera for their generosity in the loan and use of their beautiful tableware and chinaware. Choon, your creative ideas and suggestions were my inspiration as I planned for the photography session.

Special thanks to Tan Su Lyn, to whom I owe the beautiful articles written about myself and on Shanghai and Shanghainese cuisine included in this book. Thanks to Edmond Ho who brought his impressive talent as a photographer to this project. I thank him for his eye for detail and his tireless enthusiasm. Thanks also to Allan Tan for his part as Edmond's assistant.

A big "thank you" to my team at Whampoa Club, Shanghai, who assisted in the photography session above carrying out their daily duties, namely Hew Choong Yew, Jimmy Kok, Lily Wang, Pan Jia Qing, Bao Qi, Julia Shi and Chen Jun. And those whom I have inadvertently left out, thank you.

Last but not least, to all my friends and guests who have supported me through the years, without whom I would not be the person I am today—Frank Stocek, Stephane Blanc, Peter Haug, Martin Rinck, Rainer Zinngrebe, Neil Jacobs, Tracy Mercer, Joachin Tan, Ng Lang, Lee Chee Keen and Joseph Soen—I learned so much from you over the years. My heartfelt thanks to each one of you.

Foreword

"Cooking under the same roof as Jereme at Three On the Bund in Shanghai made me discover Jereme's talents as well as his dedication to his art. He is a pioneer in recreating the ancient cuisines of China and Asia for today's palates, with a healthy respect for their traditions.

The elegance and finesse of his menu make dining at his restaurant a unique experience of contrasts and textures. Whenever I am in Shanghai, I never miss a chance to put myself in his hands and dine at Whampoa Club for a truly remarkable meal."

Jean-Georges Vongerichten Chef and Restaurateur

The elegance and finesse of his menu make dining at his restaurant
a unique experience of contrasts and textures..

...a multi-faceted understanding of the Chinese kitchen has helped me in
my endeavour to create a contemporary culinary style.

Introduction

Over the few years that I have made Shanghai my home, I have been very fortunate. I have gotten to know people from all walks of life, ranging from the average man on the street to the stars and celebrities of Shanghai's elite. And no matter what their backgrounds are, the Shanghainese, as well as the people who choose to live and work in Shanghai, continue to impress me with their readiness for adventure and openness to trying out new things. In many ways, tasting the food of Shanghai has been just as eye-opening and mind-boggling for me, a person living in China for the very first time. It has been equally amazing being able to bite into a searing hot *shao mai* (glutinous rice dumpling) along the street, as it has been soaking in the cool vibes of slick, new designer restaurants in Xin Tian Di where wonderful modern Western creations are served. It's exciting to be living in a city that's quickly becoming one of the hottest in the region, if not the world, and working in the thick of things as a Chinese chef looking to satisfy an increasingly sophisticated Shanghai palate.

Chinese cooking in many parts of the world, even today, has remained fairly traditional.

My own training, starting as an apprentice at age 13 in the kitchen of my family's restaurant, New Min Ho in Hong Kong, was in old school Chinese cooking techniques which I remain faithful to today. But I have benefited from the broader perspective that a firm foundation in all four cornerstones of Chinese cookery—dim sum preparation, barbecue and roasting, wok handling, and cutting and carving—has afforded me. Most Chinese chefs specialise in just one aspect of the cuisine, but a multi-faceted understanding of the Chinese kitchen has helped me in my endeavour to create a contemporary culinary style. This is a style that improvises, not for the mere sake of creating something new, but rather to appeal to increasingly cosmopolitan diners seeking more out of the fine dining experience while respecting tradition.

I have always had a passion for exploring the roots of Chinese cuisine and have made annual pilgrimages to the different cities and regions in China in a bid to study local recipes, ingredients, culture and people. My career has also taken me to many other parts of the world where I have learnt from other dining cultures while, at the same time, sharing bits of my own. These experiences helped me approach regional Chinese cuisine with a modern touch and inspired me to apply the same approach to Shanghainese cuisine when I launched Whampoa Club (one of three dining concepts located in the sleek Michael Graves-designed Three on the Bund).

The cuisine of Shanghai is considered relatively young when compared to the eight major regional cuisines of China, traditionally identified as the food of Sichuan, Beijing, Shandong, Fujian, Jiangsu (Huaiyang), Anhui, Hunan, and Guangzhou (Canton). Shanghainese cuisine takes inspiration from many older sources and culinary traditions. Even then, much of Shanghai's glorious food traditions were lost when political instability hit in the 1930s. I took it upon myself to unearth these lost recipes by scouring through old manuscripts and publications now incomplete due to wear-and-tear. The point was not only to find out how classic dishes like drunken hairy crab, drunken chicken and lion's head were prepared, but to understand why certain ingredients were used, uncover the origins of these ingredients and discover how they may have been used in various other regional cuisines. The intention wasn't simply to master these old dishes. I believe that a chef needs to understand the fundamentals of a dish and the different uses of its components before re-interpreting it. What I have done, in this instance, is to refine the look and presentation of traditional Shanghainese dishes and introduce ingredients from all over the globe into the mix.

Some of my dishes may seem unusual, incorporating non-Chinese ingredients like foie gras or truffles, but they are very much Chinese in their provenance—the recipe and techniques are always resolutely Chinese. While I choose to showcase foie gras, traditionally considered a French ingredient, my marinating and cooking methods remain Chinese. They take inspiration from Shanghai's signature cold dish, *nuo mi hong zao*, which consists of red dates filled with glutinous rice. The result is a harmonious balance between a rich, savoury ingredient and a sweet, traditional dish. When faced with traditionally prepared drunken chicken that is often too dry, I decided to freeze the liquid the chicken is usually marinated in and shave it over the dish just before it is served. As the flavoursome ice melts over the chicken, it proffers a novel taste sensation without compromising the integrity of the original dish. It is this attention to detail, combined with creativity and a knowledge of Shanghainese and Chinese cookery, that I believe makes my culinary offerings a little different.

And in many ways, it's quite natural that Shanghainese cuisine cleaves so well to this treatment. Shanghai itself has always been the seat of change and revolution, the bridge between East and West for China, as well as the rest of the world. Through my recipes, I hope to offer readers a glimpse of where Shanghai's cuisine is headed, and show how it has established a beautiful balance between the old and the new.

Jereme Leung

The revitalised new Shanghai as we know it today, took root in the 1990s. By the mid 1990s, over a quarter of the world's high-

rise cranes could be found in this one city. Redevelopment surged forward, as it continues to do so today, at a frantic pace.

Admittedly, Shanghai's relationships with the
Western powers of the day in the mid-19th century were by no means equal,
        however, as a result of their presence, numerous modern luxuries of urban
life were introduced to the throbbing soon-to-be metropolis.

Shanghai style

There's an irresistible charm to Shanghai. It's inebriatingly exotic and effortlessly sophisticated: simultaneously oh-so Chinese, yet idiosyncratically European. The romance of its hedonistic, jazz-era pleasure dome past and the thrill of its part in jumpstarting New China into its glorious future have naturally edged the "city of the moment" title onto its mantle. To put it simply, Shanghai rocks. China's largest metropolis has, over the past two decades, started to regain its standing among the world's major cities; the Shanghainese comfortably rejoining the ranks of global trend-setters, taste arbiters and leaders of innovation. Asia's, if not the world's, fastest changing city exudes a buzz and energy that inspires even the most conservative of entrepreneurs to live out their wildest dreams (be it a business idea, building design or lifestyle concept), because in Shanghai—where a gung-ho population embraces the new and novel—dreams do come true, oftentimes in the blink of an eye. And in true Shanghainese fashion, they're only accepted when delivered hip and hot. In this city, nothing is done in halves, nor quietly and subtly. Just look out your window as night falls and witness the city's long-standing infatuation with neon lights. It's either all or nothing. New Shanghai, much like its resplendent, old, rouged-cheeked and snug *qipao*-clad self, is swiftly transfixing the world's imagination with its sass, inventiveness and elan. The glorious Paris of the East has risen like a phoenix poised to flutter her glittering wings yet again. And she's set to enthral yet another generation of the world's glitterati and literati.

The revitalised new Shanghai as we know it today, took root in the 1990s. By the mid 1990s, over a quarter of the world's high-rise cranes could be found in this one city. Redevelopment surged forward, as it continues to do so today, at a frantic pace. And investments poured into the city, virtually transforming it into one cavernous construction site—one that by the dawn of the 21st century, could proudly lay claim to a US$2 billion airport in Pudong (which was little more than swamp land a mere decade before), metro lines, light rail-lines, several convention centres, underground tunnels, plus an entire new city (said to be eight times larger than London's Canary Wharf) also in Pudong.

In fact, Pudong's eclectic, somewhat schizophrenic skyline best encapsulates what the Shanghai of the new millennium aspires to achieve, constantly reaching heavenwards with each record-making architectural statement of a skyscraper which is more often than not a marriage of Eastern and Western design precepts. Sometimes, this union is seamless, at others, bewitchingly jarring. Pudong's finest, at present, is the eye-catching 420-metre tall modern Art-Deco Jin Mao Tower (home to the Grand Hyatt) which stands out above the new city's Manhattan-eque skyline and is one of the tallest buildings in the world. Then there's the now-iconic Oriental Pearl TV Tower with its unforgettable mammoth pink and silver globes, said to be the largest structure of its kind in Asia. Its aspiration to become a city like none other inspired the world's biggest names in architecture—including Sir Norman Foster, Michael Graves and I.M. Pei—to flock to the once more seductive Pearl of the Orient. They're eager to leave their marks on the metropolis we've all come to believe is destined to become the world's next key global city, where nothing is considered too bold, too unconventional nor too forward thinking.

Of course, there are the other world's bests. Shanghai is also home to the world's fastest train (the German-built Maglev), the longest underwater pedestrian tunnel and the world's tallest hotel (the Grand Hyatt). In more ways than one, the city is truly becoming a force to be reckoned with. Yet, the throbbing dynamism that propels Shanghai as it strives to become a major city of the 21st century—a financial, cultural and intellectual hot spot—doesn't stem exclusively from the potential of its tomorrows as articulated by ultra high-tech and futuristic Pudong. Across the Huangpu River along the Bund, is the other equally enchanting face of Shanghai, one that affirms that much of Shanghai's vitality today also stems from its past. Often described as a gallery of the world's architecture, Shanghai's historic waterfront stands testament to the city's rich and colourful history. It's been said that Shanghai offers a variety of architectural offerings unrivalled by any city in the world. Along the Bund alone, awe-inspiring neoclassical, Renaissance, art deco and contemporary edifices are beautifully juxtaposed, unabashedly harking to the city's age-old dalliances with the West.

Admittedly, Shanghai's relationships with the Western powers of the day in the mid-19th century
were by no means equal, however, as a result of their presence, numerous modern luxuries of
urban life were introduced to the throbbing soon-to-be metropolis. Following the signing of the
Treaty of Nanking in 1842, Shanghai rapidly became China's leading treaty port and by 1870,
became the world's fifth largest port. The city was home to China's first banks in 1848, and
subsequently welcomed gaslight, electricity, running water and cars ahead of the rest of the country.
By the beginning of the 20th century, Shanghai already had the infrastructure of a modern city,
even by Western standards. And by the 1930s, it was on par with the largest metropolises in
the world.

Indeed, by then the world's fifth largest city was home to the tallest buildings in Asia, boasted more
cars in one city than the whole of China put together, and was a haven for more than 70,000
foreigners (out of a population of three million). The city was three times as crowded as London and
the cosmopolitan mix of people was unequalled anywhere in the world. Naturally, Shanghai became
the decadent port-of-call for the world's *crème de la crème* and luxury cruise liners were soon found

docked alongside foreign gunboats. Dramatist, actor and composer, Noel Coward arrived with 27 pieces of luggage and a gramophone, caught the flu and wrote *Private Lives* at the Cathay (now Peace) Hotel. America's Sweetheart, Mary Pickford, and her celluloid-perfect husband, Douglas Fairbanks, created a social stir, while film director Josef Von Sternberg toured the city for inspiration before directing Marlene Dietrich in *Shanghai Express*. Wallis Warfield Simpson spent a year here with her naval officer husband (King George V would later abdicate the throne of England in order to marry the divorcee). Even Bertrand Russell, Oscar Wilde, Bernard Shaw and Charlie Chaplin made their pilgrimages to this bohemian hotbed of supine pleasure and intellectual vitality.

It's the magic of this Shanghai that we continue to seek even today, when we eagerly touchdown at the ultra sleek and modern Pudong Airport. We yearn for that deliciously decadent metropolis where the elite sipped on gin and tonic at the utterly colonial Shanghai Club surrounded by jazz musicians and Siberian acrobats; where life felt like a constant merry-go-round of parties and balls, dinners at the club and tea dances at the Astor. Life in Shanghai was fabulous for the wealthy. It offered an endless abundance of amusement. There were sexy cabarets where a different foreign band sang each night and glamorous jazz-palaces filled with head-turning couples dancing the foxtrot. In teahouses, Chinese hostesses sang for their guests in classic falsetto, while over in French Concession Russian cafes, revellers indulged in cheap vodka and caviar. Then there were the glitzy nightclubs and casinos, and the mesmerising trips to the movies. It mustn't be forgotten that Shanghai's plushest theatres, the Lyceum, Grand, Lyric, Empire, Odeon and Apollo rivalled America's grandest. They were just as magnificent and breathtakingly opulent. And the cosmopolitan Shanghainese actually got to view Hollywood releases even before they reached the American heartland. It's the seduction of this Shanghai, perhaps best embodied by the calendar girls of the era in their come-hither poses and scandalously tight *qipao*, that proves profoundly irresistible. After all, the figure skimming dress with the high Mandarin collar that we now consider inherently Chinese was really an iconic fashion trend that took off in the 1910s and 1920s after Shanghainese screen sirens adopted it as their preferred on- and off-screen attire. The *qipao*, as we know it today, was the global-minded, outward-looking Shanghainese elite's response to European ladies' fashion. This still-vibrant metropolis is no stranger to the boundary-blurring, East-West culture-fusing effects of being a global centre. And most admirably, the Shanghainese seem to embrace it.

The spirit of change and openness has long been part of the bedrock of Shanghai. The city has always been the place where controversies over the latest ideas in politics, art and literature raged. It was in Shanghai, in 1919, that the New Culture Movement, a powerful literary and social revolution that called for the sweeping away of outmoded aspects of Chinese life, gained momentum. Among its proponents were Chinese literature's biggest names, including Mao Dun, Ba Jin and Lu Xun. At the dinner table, Shanghai is considered to have developed the most eclectic of China's cuisines, incorporating dishes and ingredients not only from all over the country, but also from the West. This could only be due to the adventurous and adaptive tastebuds of Shanghai's diners. Fellow Chinese looked to Shanghai, and continue to do so, to pick up the world's swishest new trends. The city has been attributed with diffusing the gastronomic hallmarks of the British, French and Russians throughout the rest of China with the bread, cakes, pies and snacks of its colonial past. And in its heyday in the early 20th century, the opulence and majesty of Shanghai's renowned restaurants, like

3-6-9 and the Winter Garden, were only matched by the splendour of its lush jazz palaces, theatres and hotels. These restaurants catered to the top-most elite and served lavish banquets that would run up to tens of thousands of dollars in today's currency.

As we enter a new millennium, the Shanghainese are re-establishing their presence on the international restaurant scene, harnessing their natural talent for fashioning spectacular, larger-than-life paeans to pleasure. Dining in Shanghai is an exhilarating experience because whether you're people watching at M on the Bund, delighting in slivers of century egg slathered in caviar at Whampoa Club, jostling with families at Bao Luo or steeping yourself in Zen minimalism at Shintori, you're left in no doubt that you're in Shanghai. It's in the energy, the ambience and the people. Each dining destination may be dazzlingly different and stupendously stylish, yet it's the frisson that the city thrillingly creates—as it almost casually melds a pinch of the East with a dash of the West, a measure of history with a shot of the future—that is so unique and intoxicating.

It is only natural that a contemporary Chinese, new Shanghainese gustatory revolution should take seed in this city of acute contrast and sublime fusion. The desire to push the envelope, without losing its sense of self, has always been at the heart of this city's feisty spirit. Shanghai is a city like no other. It possesses an aesthetic, a style, a way of living that enraptures both heart and mind. To sup at Shanghai's table is to savour the pleasures of life itself.

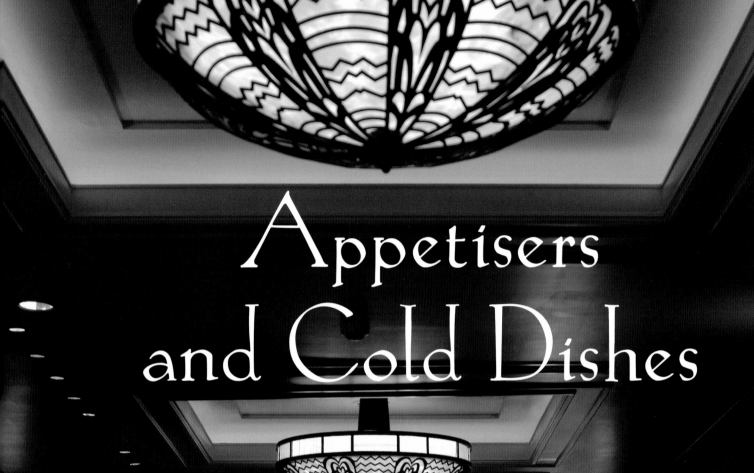

Appetisers and Cold Dishes

The Shanghainese meal is simply incomplete if it doesn't commence with a selection of cold dishes washed down with a hot cup of tea or cold glass of beer.

Even at street stalls and the most humble of dining establishments, you'll find platters piled high with *xun yu* (soy-braised smoked fish), *xun dan* (tea-smoked duck eggs), *gui hua tang ou* (candied lotus root with glutinous rice and Osmanthus blossoms) and *kao fu* (wheat gluten, often paired with black fungus and *enokitake* mushrooms) on display. While at other restaurants, a cart laden with a little of everything might be brought directly to the table where diners will often select three to four dishes, always mindful of maintaining a balance between seafood, meat, vegetables and bean curd or gluten.

Unlike the usual banquet offerings of stereotypical Chinese banquets, Shanghai's incomparable plethora of cold dishes (most often featuring soy sauce and sugar, the hallmarks of Shanghainese cuisine) are intricately sophisticated culinary creations filled with complex layers of flavour— especially since it has also adopted and adapted many of the specialities enjoyed in neighbouring provinces, often using them as the basis for the city's own tantalising starters. From Suzhou and Hangzhou, Shanghai has acquired the taste for *zheng jiang xiao rou* (pork jelly) and *yang gao* (lamb jelly) which are most often enjoyed with a dip of finely shredded ginger and black vinegar. Ningbo, just hours away from Shanghai, has contributed its famous *zao* technique, one that involves using a cold marinade flavoured with glutinous rice wine brine.

The Shanghainese have fashioned delicious *zao*-based cold dishes incorporating ingredients such as fish, shellfish, snails, bamboo shoots and even hairy broad beans. Never a people to shy away from the exotic, they've even embraced raw dishes, another rarity in most other Chinese cuisines. Apart for the city's renowned drunken crab—a must-try for all first-time visitors to Shanghai—there's also *chiang he xia* where live river prawns are soaked in a heady *zao* marinade. Truly, no other region in China takes such pride in its cold dishes.

sugar-cured glutinous red dates with cinnamon apple and seared goose liver

serves 4 / preparation time: 30 minutes / cooking time: 40 minutes

INGREDIENTS

Celery	150 g, sliced
Fresh lily bulbs	150 g

glutinous red dates

Glutinous rice flour	50 g
Instant milk powder	50 g
Warm water	60 ml
Sun-dried red dates (seedless)	200 g, about 40
Sugar	500 g
Water	250 ml

goose liver

Goose liver	120 g
Freshly ground black pepper	a dash
Sesame oil	$1/2$ tsp
Coriander (cilantro) leaves	2 sprigs, minced
Garlic	1 clove, peeled and minced
Shallot	1 clove, peeled and minced

cinnamon apple

Green apple	1, about 100 g
Ground cinnamon	a dash

METHOD

- Prepare glutinous red dates. Combine glutinous rice flour and milk powder with warm water. Knead into a soft dough and dice.

- Make a slit on each red date and fill with a dice of dough.

- In a deep pot, melt 490 g sugar with water over low heat. Place red dates in and simmer for 30 minutes until soft and cooked. Remove pot from heat and leave dates to soak in syrup. Set aside.

- Prepare goose liver. Remove visible clotted blood, veins and membranes from goose liver. Slice into 5 × 1-cm pieces. Marinate with black pepper, sesame oil, coriander, garlic, shallot and remaining sugar from glutinous red dates. Heat a pan and sear goose liver just before serving.

- Prepare cinnamon apple. Pare skin off green apple and cut apple into small 1-cm cubes.

- In a non-stick pan, add apple cubes and some syrup from cooking glutinous red dates. Simmer for 5 minutes until apple cubes are soft. Sprinkle ground cinnamon over.

- Place glutinous red dates on a serving plate. Top with celery and fresh lily bulbs, followed by pan-seared goose liver. Garnish with fried ginger shreds if desired and serve immediately.

chilled drunken chicken topped with shaved *shao xing* wine ice

serves 4 / preparation time: 30 minutes / marinating time: 24 hours

INGREDIENTS

Ginkgo nuts	50 g
Edamame beans	50 g
Chinese wolfberries	10 g
Fresh lily bulbs	50 g

chicken

Water	1.5 litres
Spring onions (scallions)	5
Ginger	5 slices, each 0.2-cm thick
Shao xing wine	5 Tbsp
Free range chicken	1, about 1.4 kg

marinade

Water	1 litre
Spring onions (scallions)	5
Ginger	5 slices, each 0.2-cm thick
Sugar	1 Tbsp
Star anise	2
Cinnamon sticks	2, each 3-cm long
Bay leaves	4
Salt	40 g
Shao xing wine	300 ml
Chinese rice wine	2 tsp

METHOD

- Prepare marinade. Bring water to the boil and add in spring onions, ginger, sugar, star anise, cinnamon, bay leaves and salt. Lower heat and simmer for 3 minutes. Remove from heat and allow to cool before adding *shao xing* wine and rice wine.

- Strain and reserve half the marinade for soaking chicken. Place other half in the freezer until frozen.

- Prepare chicken. Bring water to the boil and add in spring onions, ginger and *shao xing* wine. Lower heat and simmer chicken for 15–20 minutes until cooked. Remove and immediately soak poached chicken in ice water to cool it down. Debone chicken and place in reserved marinade. Leave for at least 24 hours in the chiller.

- Remove bitter centre of ginkgo nuts and blanch together with edamame beans and wolfberries until cooked. Drain and combine with fresh lily bulbs. Divide into 4 equal servings and place into martini glasses.

- Cut chicken into small pieces and place into prepared martini glasses. Shave frozen chicken marinade over chicken. Serve immediately.

chef's note: Free range chickens (*tu ji*) are allowed to roam freely in the farms, so they have firmer fresh. When used in double-boiled soups, the thin layer of fat under their skin gives the soup an excellent aroma.

live river prawns in preserved bean curd sauce

serves 4 / preparation time: 15 minutes / cooking time: 5 minutes

INGREDIENTS

Live river prawns
(shrimps)   250 g

marinade

Preserved
red bean curd   100 g
Sugar   40 g
Light soy sauce   30 ml
Ginger   1-cm knob, peeled
Spring onion
(scallion)   1
Garlic   1 clove, peeled
Shao xing wine   20 ml
Chinese white wine   10 ml (see *chef's note*)
Ground white
pepper   a dash

METHOD

- Combine all marinade ingredients in a blender (food processor) then sieve and reserve liquid.

- Place prawns in an ice bath to put them to sleep. Cut away spears and legs and wash well. Drain.

- Pour marinade onto prepared prawns. Cover and leave to marinate for 5 minutes before serving.

chef's note: Shanghai river prawns and fresh water baby prawns are usually about 5-cm long. They have soft shells and are ideal served raw. It is essential that these prawns are live when preparing this dish.

Chinese white wine is usually made using rice, malt and barley. It has a higher alcohol content (up to 60%) than wines made from glutinous rice, such as *shao xing* wine (11–15%). White wines with a high alcohol content is preferred for this dish.

shanghainese tea-smoked eggs topped with sevruga caviar

serves 4 / preparation time: 15 minutes / cooking time: 10 minutes

INGREDIENTS

Duck eggs (red yolk)	3
Fine salt	1 tsp or a few drops of vinegar
Sevruga caviar	50 g

for smoking

Red tea leaves	20 g
Sugar	1 Tbsp
Rice	20 g
Five-spice powder	$1/6$ tsp
Plain (all-purpose) flour	20 g
Aluminium foil	1 sheet, about 30 x 30-cm

METHOD

- Fill a deep pot with enough water to totally submerge eggs. Place duck eggs in and bring to the boil. (Adding in 1 tsp salt or a few drops of vinegar to the boiling liquid will help prevent the eggshell from sticking to the white of the egg, making it easier to peel.)

- When water comes to the boil, wait for 1 minute before removing from heat. Cover pot and leave eggs in hot water for 5 minutes. Remove eggs and place immediately into an ice bath to cool.

- Peel shells off carefully when eggs are cold enough to handle.

- Prepare smoking ingredients. Soak tea leaves in water for 3 minutes, then drain and combine with sugar, rice, five-spice powder and flour.

- Place aluminium foil in wok and ensure that it is large enough to cover the bottom of the wok. Place smoking ingredients on foil and stand a rack over.

- Place peeled eggs on rack and heat wok until yellow smoke rises. Cover and smoke eggs for 1 minute. Remove eggs and discard smoking ingredients.

- Slice smoked duck eggs into halves and top with sevruga caviar. Serve immediately.

chef's note: This is a classic Shanghainese dish that requires the egg white to be cooked while leaving the yolk fluid. This dish was traditionally served with a sprinkle of salt. I have used caviar to offer the same level of saltiness, but with an additional sensation of flavours.

photograph on pg 41

soy braised brown wheat gluten
with dried lily buds and mushrooms

serves 6 / preparation time: 10 minutes / cooking time: 45 minutes

INGREDIENTS

Brown wheat gluten	500 g
Cooking oil	300 ml
Shallot oil*	100 ml
Bay leaves	3
Star anise	50 g
Cinnamon sticks	50 g
Basic stock	500 ml (see pg 175)
Dried Chinese mushrooms	50 g, soaked to soften and sliced
Dried lily buds	50 g
Peanuts (groundnuts)	50 g
Light soy sauce	100 ml
Dark soy sauce	a dash
Sugar	200 g
Sesame oil	100 ml

*shallot oil

Cooking oil	300 ml
Shallots	80 g, peeled
Garlic	30 g, peeled
Ginger	20 g, peeled
Spring onion (scallion)	1

METHOD

- Prepare shallot oil. Heat oil over medium heat and fry shallots, garlic, ginger and spring onion until golden brown. Strain oil and discard ingredients. Leave oil to cool before storing in a clean, covered container at room temperature. Use as required

- Tear or cut brown wheat gluten into serving sizes. (It was traditionally believed that in order for the wheat gluten to absorb the flavours of the seasoning, it should be torn apart by hand and not sliced with a knife.)

- Bring a pot of water to the boil and add some salt. Blanch wheat gluten for 5 minutes until soft and cooked. Drain.

- Heat cooking oil over medium heat and deep-fry wheat gluten in batches until crispy on the outside and soft in the inner part. Drain.

- In a deep pot, heat shallot oil over low heat and lightly fry bay leaves, star anise and cinnamon sticks until aroma is released. Add all remaining ingredients and simmer for 45 minutes over low heat, stirring constantly to prevent ingredients from sticking to the bottom of the pot.

- Garnish and serve warm, sprinkled with a little sesame oil if desired.

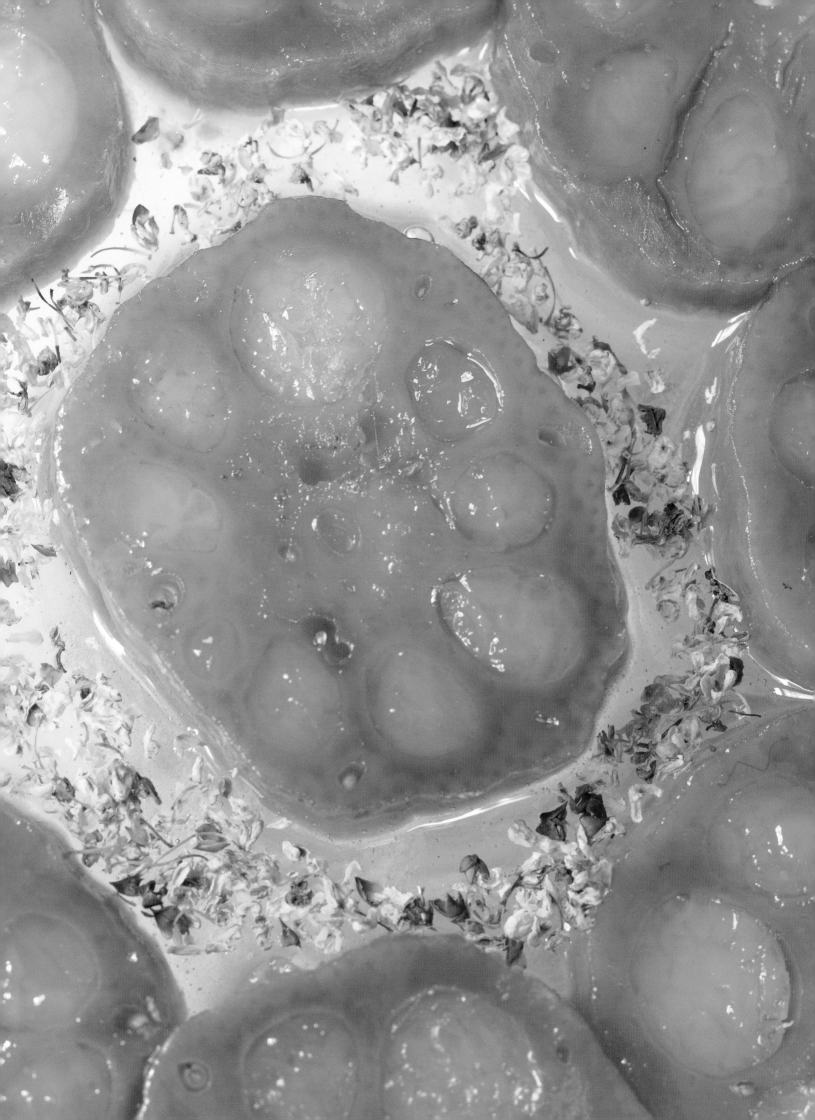

osmanthus candied lotus root filled with slow-cooked glutinous grains

serves 4 / preparation time: 30 minutes / cooking time: 6 hours

INGREDIENTS

Lotus root	500 g
Glutinous rice	150 g, soaked in water for 15 minutes
Cocktail sticks	10
Water	1.5 litres
Cane sugar	200 g, sliced
Rock sugar	200 g
Sugar	200 g
Dried Osmanthus blossoms	1 tsp
Honey	2 tsp

METHOD

- Scrape skin off lotus root. Cut 1.5-cm off the top of root and reserve for use as a cover.

- Fill cavity of lotus root with drained glutinous rice and pack as tightly as possible using a chopstick. Fill the lotus root cap with glutinous rice as well and secure it back in place using cocktail sticks.

- Bring water to the boil and add all 3 sugars and $1/2$ tsp Osmanthus blossoms.

- Overturn a small plate and place it at the bottom of the pot. Place a bamboo net over the plate. This will prevent the lotus root from sticking to the pot during cooking.

- Place lotus root into the pot and lower heat to simmer for 6 hours until lotus root is soft and well-cooked.

- Drain and allow to cool then cut into serving slices. Drizzle with honey and garnish with remaining dried Osmanthus blossoms.

old-fashioned shanghai smoked fish

serves 4 / preparation time: 20 minutes / cooking time: 40 minutes

INGREDIENTS

Ginger	20 g, peeled and finely chopped
Shallots	20 g, peeled and finely chopped
Spring onions (scallions)	20 g, finely chopped
Shao xing wine	100 ml
Light soy sauce	150 ml
Grey mullet fillet	1, about 1 kg, cut into 2-cm thick slices
Cooking oil	2 litres
Star anise	2
Cassia bark	2-cm length
Bay leaves	2
Water	100 ml
Rock sugar	100 g
Sugar	100 g
Shanghai soy sauce	100 ml
Sesame oil	50 ml
Ground white pepper	a dash

garnish

Roasted white sesame seeds

METHOD

- Combine ginger, shallots and spring onions with 50 ml *shao xing* wine and 50 ml light soy sauce. Marinate fish fillet for about 20 minutes.

- Remove ginger, shallot and spring onions from fish marinade and drain. Heat a wok with some cooking oil and sauté drained ginger, shallot and spring onions, star anise, cassia and bay leaves until fragrant.

- Add water and remaining ingredients except cooking oil. Bring to the boil then lower heat and simmer for 20 minutes, constantly stirring until a thick sauce is formed.

- Heat remaining cooking oil over medium-high heat and deep-fry fish fillet until cooked. Maintain a high oil temperature to achieve a crispy exterior and moist inner flesh. Drain and immediately soak fish fillet in thickened sauce to coat well. Serve with sauce and roasted sesame seeds. Garnish as desired.

chef's note: Shanghai soy sauce is more complex in flavour compared to other soy sauces because it is infused with spices such as Sichuan peppercorns, star anise, cinnamon, cloves and sometimes even chilli, ginger and onions.

baby yellow fin fish roulade poached in rice wine brine

serves 3 / preparation time: 45 minutes / marinating time: 12 hours

INGREDIENTS

Yellow fin fish	3, each about 200 g
Cooking oil	1 litre
Flying fish roe	1 tsp
Sevruga caviar	1 tsp
Spring onion (scallion) tips	6

fish marinade

Water	500 ml
Salt	$^1/_8$ tsp
Sugar	$^1/_2$ tsp
Spring onions (scallions)	5
Ginger	5 slices, each 0.2-cm thick
Star anise	2
Cassia bark	2-cm piece
Bay leaves	5
Shao xing wine	20 ml
Rice wine brine	40 ml

METHOD

- Prepare fish marinade. Bring water to the boil and add salt, sugar, spring onions and ginger. Transfer liquid to a deep container and add star anise, cassia and bay leaves. Allow mixture to cool completely before adding *shao xing* wine and rice wine brine.

- Prepare fish roulade. Scale yellow fin fish and remove bones to get 2 fillets from each fish. Roll fillets up with skin facing inwards. Lightly steam fish roulades over medium heat to firm shape. Allow to cool.

- Heat oil over medium heat and deep-fry roulades until light golden brown in colour.

- Place fried fish roulades into fish marinade and soak for at least 12 hours in the refrigerator.

- Remove fish roulades from marinade and drain of excessive liquid.

- Top fish roulades with flying fish roe and caviar. Garnish with spring onion tips. If desired, the fish marinade can be lightly thickened with a little corn flour (cornstarch) and served as a sauce.

chef's note: Rice wine brine (*zao lu*) is a Shanghai and Ningbo regional specialty. It is usually made by fermenting rice with a variety of Chinese spices, then distilled to produce a fragrant brine. Rice wine brine is commonly used to marinate cold appetisers from the Zhejiang region.

photograph on pg 49

drunken hairy crab and sweet prawn tartar

As this dish is served raw, it is important that the hairy crab is live and the ebi is extremely fresh.

serves 1 / preparation time: 10 minutes / marinating time: 48 hours

INGREDIENTS

Female hairy crab	1, about 150 g
Ebi (sweet prawns (shrimps))	5

marinade

Ginger	100 g, peeled and finely chopped
Japanese soy sauce	40 ml
Sugar	60 g
Dark soy sauce	10 ml
Zheng jiang vinegar	50 ml
Chang jiang black vinegar	50 ml

METHOD

- Prepare marinade. In a clean non-stick pan, sauté ginger until fragrant. Add Japanese soy sauce and sugar. Bring to the boil stirring, to ensure sugar melts and mixture is well blended. Remove from heat and add remaining marinade ingredients. Allow to cool.

- Clean hairy crab under running water and pat-dry. Place in marinade and refrigerate for at least 48 hours for best results. After marinating, remove as much shell from crab as possible and cut it into serving sizes. Place in a small serving bowl.

- Peel ebi, leaving only 1 ebi with a tail for better presentation. Lightly chop remaining ebi into chunks. (Do not chop too finely as ebi will lose its bite.) Place ebi on top of hairy crab and sprinkle marinade over sparingly.

- Place bowl into a larger bowl filled with crushed ice to keep dish chilled. Serve immediately with a small serving of wasabi if desired.

Soups

Soups have a special nurturing and comforting quality
about them that transcends cuisines and cultures.
The double-boiled and simmered soups of Shanghai are no different.

Each porcelain soup-spoonful of hearty flavour not only satiates the hunger of the body, but also enfolds the heart with a loving blanket of comfort.

At the core of Shanghainese cuisine are two cooking traditions. *hai pai cai* is associated with the old eateries, like De Xing Guan, that lined the Bund back in the days when it was teeming with coolies labouring over tonnes of cargo. The food they served was tailored to the needs of diners who spent their entire day exerting their bodies, so dishes were wholesome and had a high salt content (in order to replenish the inordinate quantities of salt they lost through perspiration). And because the coolies hailed from many different parts of China, Shanghainese chefs learnt to introduce regional ingredients and flavours that appealed to their myriad customers. The resulting cuisine is a fusion of sorts.

In Shanghainese homes, on the other hand, *jia chang cai* took root. Dishes were simple and seasonal, consisting of whatever ingredients were easily available. The common thread that binds both traditions is the uncomplicated, peasant-style approach to food. So, unlike the elaborate superior stocks of Southern Chinese culinary traditions, Shanghai's soups are often filled with ingredients of humble origins. Yet, while they may appear ordinary (in truth, the cuisine is not renowned for its soups), you'll quickly realise that their rich and intense melding of flavours leaves an unforgettable impression on the palate. Drawing from this peasant tradition is *yan du xian*, a rustic broth made with pig innards, air-dried bamboo shoots and salted pork. Although it is a classic, it now makes such rare appearances on menus that it's difficult to taste one in Shanghai itself. The simplicity of the ingredients used to make *kou shan si*, another regional speciality, belies the refinement of the elegant soup. A fragrant and utterly pure chicken consommé is first coaxed into being through hours of careful double-boiling. The stunningly flavourful broth is then served with chicken, ham and bamboo shoots — all cut so minutely and uniformly that it becomes a challenge to tell each ingredient apart.

braised golden coin shark's fin with crab roe cream

serves 1 / preparation time: 20 minutes / cooking time: 12 hours

INGREDIENTS

Golden coin shark's fin	80 g
Cooking oil	2 tsp
Ginger	1-cm knob, peeled and minced
Superior stock	180 ml (see pg 175)
Shao xing wine	1 tsp
Sugar	to taste
Salt	to taste
Ground white pepper	a dash
Hairy crabmeat	50 g (see *chef's note*)
Hairy crab roe	30 g (see *chef's note*)
Potato flour	2 tsp, mixed with some water
Egg white	$^1/_2$

METHOD

- Steam shark's fin for 4 hours then soak in a little cold water overnight. Leave shark's fin in soaking liquid and steam for 2 hours until soft. Drain and set aside (see *chef's note*).

- Heat oil in a wok and sauté minced ginger until fragrant, then add superior stock, *shao xing* wine, sugar, salt and pepper, prepared shark's fin, crabmeat and roe. Thicken mixture with potato flour solution and finish by stirring in egg white. Serve immediately.

chef's note: Golden coin shark's fin is from the dogfish shark. It is so-named because of the many round patterns on the fin that resembles coins. This type of shark's fin is favoured for its tenderness as it usually from young sharks.

Pre-cooked shark's fin is commonly available in many Asian seafood specialty stores. Good quality shark's fin will not melt or dissolve into the stock easily when boiled. If it does, the fins were treated with food additives like lye water (*jian shui*).

To prepare hairy crabmeat and roe, place live hairy crabs in an ice bath to put them to sleep. Then, steam them for 15 minutes until cooked. Allow to cool and carefully shell crabs. Remove crabmeat and roe. This mixture is also known as hairy crab powder in Shanghai.

hairy crab glutinous dumplings in golden broth

serves 6 / preparation time: 30 minutes / cooking time: 3 hours

INGREDIENTS

filling

Cooking oil	1 Tbsp
Finely chopped ginger	1 tsp
Pork skin jelly	25 g (see *chef's note*, pg 153)
Hairy crabmeat and roe	350 g (see *chef's note*, pg 54)
Salt	to taste
Shao xing wine	75 ml
Sugar	to taste
Ground white pepper	a dash
Sesame oil	a few drops
Potato flour	2 tsp

dumplings

Glutinous rice flour	150 g
Vegetable shortening	50 g
Wheat starch flour	38 g
Water	3 Tbsp
Water or egg white for brushing	
White sesame seeds	1 Tbsp

golden broth

Stewing hen	1, about 1 kg
Duck	1, about 1 kg
Pork knuckles	450 g, chopped
Water	5 litres
White peppercorns	1 tsp
Tangerine peel	2-cm square piece
Ginger	30 g
Spring onions (scallions)	30 g
Carrots	500 g
Ground white pepper	a dash
Salt	to taste

METHOD

- Prepare filling. Heat oil in a wok and sauté finely chopped ginger until fragrant. Add pork skin jelly with hairy crabmeat and roe. Season with salt, *shao xing* wine, sugar, pepper and sesame oil. Thicken mixture with potato flour and refrigerate. The mixture should set into a jelly once cooled completely.

- Prepare dumplings. Combine glutinous rice flour with vegetable shortening, wheat starch flour and water. Knead mixture into a dough. Divide dough into 20 equal portions. Roll each portion into a 1.5-cm ball. Flatten each portion and top with filling. Enclose filling and roll into round dumplings.

- Brush 5 dumplings with some water or egg white. Coat evenly with white sesame seeds and set aside.

- Prepare golden broth. Blanch stewing hen, duck and pork knuckles in hot water for 2 minutes to remove impurities. Drain and set aside. In a deep pot, heat 5 litres water and add peppercorns, tangerine peel, ginger and spring onions. Bring to the boil then lower heat and simmer for about 2 hours 30 minutes.

- While waiting, chop carrots. Combine with a little water and blend (process) into carrot puree. Add puree to simmering broth and boil for another 30 minutes until broth turns golden in colour and flavours are fully released. Strain mixture and season to taste with pepper and salt.

- Boil remaining glutinous rice dumplings in hot water until cooked. The cooked dumplings will float to the surface. In another pot, heat some oil over medium heat and fry sesame-coated dumplings until golden brown. Drain well.

- Reheat golden broth and ladle into serving bowls. Place 3 dumplings and 1 sesame-coated dumpling into each bowl. Serve immediately.

yan du xian bamboo shoot consommé with salted and fresh pork

serves 4 / preparation time: 20 minutes / cooking time: 2 hours

Ingredients

Fresh pork belly	500 g, cut into 6 x 2-cm pieces
Air-dried salted pork belly	150 g, cut into 6 x 2-cm pieces
Water	4 litres
Spring onions (scallions)	20 g
Yellow chives	5
Ginger	30 g, peeled
Fresh spring bamboo shoots	300 g, peeled and cut into 6-cm lengths
Bai ye bean curd skin	8 sheets, each about 40 g, tied into knots
Sugar	to taste
Shao xing wine	2 tsp
Ground white pepper	a dash

METHOD

- Blanch fresh and air-dried pork in hot water for 3 minutes. Drain and discard liquid.

- Add 4 litres water to a deep pot and bring to the boil. Add in fresh and air-dried pork, spring onions, yellow chives and ginger. Boil for 30 minutes over high heat. When stock has turned white and milky, add in bamboo shoots. Lower heat and simmer for 1 hour 30 minutes. Add *bai ye* bean curd knots.

- Strain ingredients from stock. Make bundles consisting of a *bai ye* bean curd knots, bamboo shoots, and air-dried or fresh pork belly and tie with spring onions or chives as shown.

- Place bundles into deep serving plates. Reheat soup, season with sugar, *shao xing* wine and pepper. Ladle over bundles and serve immediately.

chef's note: Salt is not used in this recipe as the salt content in the air-dried pork is sufficient to flavour this tasty soup.

double-boiled free range chicken clear consommé served with truffle dumplings

serves 6 / preparation time: 30 minutes / cooking time: 3 hours

INGREDIENTS

consommé

Free range chicken	1, about 1.5 kg
Water	1.5 litres
Ginger	2-cm knob, peeled and finely chopped
Spring onion (scallion)	1, lightly bruised
Sugar	to taste
Salt	to taste

filling

Prawn (shrimp) meat	450 g
Scallops	450 g
Water chestnuts	100 g, peeled
Potato flour	1 tsp
Salt	to taste
Sugar	to taste
Ground white pepper	a dash
Shallot oil	1 Tbsp (see page 43)
Sesame oil	a dash

dough

Plain (all-purpose) flour	300 g
Water	15 ml
Vegetable shortening	80 g
Squid ink	3 drops
Black truffle powder	1 tsp
Freshly shaved black truffle	12 slices

METHOD

- Prepare consommé. Clean free range chicken, discard head and bottom. Chop chicken into 5-cm pieces and blanch in hot water for 30 seconds to remove any impurities. Wash and drain.

- Place chicken pieces in a large double-boiler with all consommé ingredients. Cover pot and double-boil for 3 hours. Remove ginger and spring onion and use a spoon to skim away the layer of chicken fat covering the surface of the consommé. Set aside.

- Prepare filling. Chop prawns and scallops into small bits. Chop water chestnuts into bits of the same size and mix with prawns and scallops. Lightly freeze filling for about 20 minutes. This will make the filling firmer and easier to handle.

- Add potato flour to chilled filling and stir well in one direction. Mix in salt, sugar and pepper, then shallot oil and sesame oil. Set aside.

- Prepare dough. Combine flour with water and vegetable shortening. Knead to form a smooth dough. Divide into 2 portions and add a few drops of squid ink and black truffle powder to 1 portion.

- Divide each dough portion into 12 equal pieces. There should be 24 pieces in all. Roll into balls and flatten with a rolling pin. Top with some filling and fold into half-moon shapes.

- Combine 2 dumplings, 1 coloured and 1 plain, to form a round shape. Secure by folding them together at the 2 corners. Press some filling into the centre joint of the dumplings. Wrap a heatproof (flameproof) plate with cling wrap and spread dumplings evenly on it. Steam dumplings for 5 minutes or until cooked.

- Make a small slit at the centre of the filling pressed between the joint of the dumplings. Insert a slice of black truffle.

- Reheat chicken consommé and pour around warm dumplings. Garnish with a edamame beans if desired. Serve hot.

double-boiled *jin shan gou* shark's fin with jinhua ham

serves 1 / preparation time: 20 minutes / cooking time: 12 hours

INGREDIENTS

Jin shan gou shark's fin	120 g
Wo sun shoots	80 g
Jinhua air-dried pork knuckle	5 slices, each about 15 g
Cooking oil	1 tsp
Superior stock	180 ml (see pg 175)
Salt	to taste
Sugar	to taste
Shao xing wine	2 tsp

METHOD

- Steam shark's fin for 4 hours then soak in cold water overnight. Leave shark's fin in soaking liquid and steam for 2 hours until soft. Drain and set aside. (See *chef's note*, pg 54.)

- Remove leaves and peel off hard skin from *wo sun* shoots, keeping only the light green stem. Cut into thin rounds about 0.5-cm thick and sauté with a little oil, salt and water until cooked.

- Reheat pork knuckle slices by steaming. (See *chef's note*.)

- Place steamed pork knuckle slices on a plate to form a circle. Place *wo sun* shoots on top followed by shark's fin. Place in a steamer to reheat.

- Heat oil in a wok and add superior stock. Season with salt, sugar and *shao xing* wine. Pour over shark's fin and serve immediately.

chef's note: *Jin shan gou* shark's fin is from a species of shark with large fins. Many up-market Chinese restaurants use this type of fin for its longer and thicker gelatin-like threads.

To slice Jinhua air-dried pork knuckle, first roast the knuckle until the outer skin forms a crust. Slice and discard the outer skin. Submerge knuckle in water and steam for 3–4 hours until it is soft enough to cut. Allow to cool before cutting into slices about 15 g each. Wrap slices and store in the chiller. It will keep for up to a few months.

shanghai's hot and sour soup

serves 1 / preparation time: 20 minutes / cooking time: 10 minutes

INGREDIENTS

Live tiger prawns (shrimps)	3
Cooking oil	2 tsp
Hot bean paste	1 Tbsp
Basic stock	180 ml (see pg 175)
Shao xing wine	1 tsp
Ground white pepper	to taste
Sugar	to taste
Salt	to taste
Bamboo shoots	10 g, cut into 3 x 0.5-cm strips
Wood ear fungus	10 g, soaked to soften and cut into 3 x 0.5-cm strips
Scallops	10 g, cut into 3 x 0.5-cm strips
Dried Chinese mushrooms	10 g, soaked to soften and cut into 3 x 0.5-cm strips
Silken bean curd	10 g, cut into 3 x 0.5-cm strips
Zhen jiang vinegar	1 Tbsp
Potato flour	15 g, mixed with some water

METHOD

- Put prawns in an ice bath to put them to sleep. Pluck heads and peel off shells, leaving only tails intact.

- Heat oil in a wok and sauté hot bean paste until aroma is released. Add stock and shao hsing wine, and pepper, sugar and salt to taste.

- Bring stock to the boil and add bamboo shoots, wood ear fungus, scallops, dried Chinese mushrooms and bean curd. Return to the boil and thicken mixture with potato starch solution.

- Remove from heat and add vinegar. Prolonged heating of Chinese vinegar causes it to lose its aroma and flavour. It is also harder to adjust the taste of the stock initially when it is heated.

- Pour soup into a serving dish and arrange tiger prawns on top. Garnish as desired and serve hot.

Seafood

Between late September and December each year, a seafood obsession grips Shanghai.

It's *da zha xie* (hairy crab) season. At their peak, the sweet, succulent flesh and lush, creamy roe of Shanghai's hairy crabs are beyond compare. At home, families will savour the much-adored delicacy steamed with ginger and spring onions, then served with shredded ginger and vinegar. Another favourite is *chao nian gao*, a dish of chopped crab fried with slivers of Shanghai rice cakes. At the finer restaurants, chefs will create luxurious and utterly indulgent *xie yan* (crab feasts)—five to six artful courses showcasing the hairy crab. Enjoy drunken crab, crab wontons, *xie fen xiao long bao* (the delicate, juicy pork dumplings Shanghai is renowned for made even more irresistible with the addition of hairy crabmeat), *chao xie jiao* (the firmer flesh of the crab leg sauteed with asparagus) and the glittering jewel in the crown, *xie fen yu ci* (hairy crab meat with shark's fin). At Whampoa Club, we've edged the crab feast up a notch or two by reinterpreting these traditional dishes, introducing exciting new gustatory counterpoints, such as sea urchin paired with old-fashioned sauteed hairy crab powder flavoured with vinegar and served in an elegant eggshell.

The bounteous selection of sensationally fresh seasonal seafood sold in the markets of Shanghai makes the prospect of such culinary invention thrilling. As the buzz at Tong Chuan Lu Seafood Wholesale Market peaks in the afternoon, the variety of seafood laid out for sale is breathtaking. Amid the hustle and bustle, you will spot fresh *he xia* (freshwater prawns), *ji yu* (crucian carp), *tang li yu* (freshwater carp), *jia yu* (turtle) and the many fresh water and deep sea delicacies from the Yangtze delta and nearby Jiangsu, Hangzhou and Suzhou. Of note too, are the species found solely where fresh water meets the sea such as *dao yu* (knife fish) between March and April when it begins its journey West to breed at the mouth of the Yangtze River. From further afield come Chilean seabass, lobster, sturgeon and geoduck. Assembled, they glisten like precious ocean jewels, impressing even the most well travelled and seasoned sushi chef.

oven-baked black cod fillet with spring onions and pickled cucumber carpaccio

serves 4 / preparation time: 20 minutes / cooking time: 30 minutes

INGREDIENTS

Black cod fillet	400 g, cut into 4 pieces, each 100 g
Spring onions (scallions)	120 g
Cooking oil	500 ml

seasoning

Potato flour	1 tsp
Sugar	1 tsp
Shallots	2
Garlic	1
Shao xing wine	2 tsp
Sesame oil	1 tsp
Hot bean paste	2 Tbsp

pickled cucumbers

Bird's eye chillies	2
Sugar	150 g
Salt	60 g
Water	100 ml
White vinegar	60 ml
Small cucumbers	100 g

METHOD

- Prepare pickled cucumbers. Make small slits on chillies and place into a pot with sugar, $^1/_4$ tsp salt and water. Bring to the boil then leave to cool to room temperature before adding vinegar. Set aside.

- Select cucumbers of similar size when buying. Slice off and discard both ends of cucumbers then mix with remaining salt. Leave for 30 minutes then rinse away salt by washing cucumbers under running water for 15–20 minutes. Pat dry and add to cooled vinegar solution. Leave overnight before serving if possible.

- Marinate cod with combined seasoning ingredients and leave refrigerated for about 1 hour.

- Use a bamboo net as a base and place a layer of spring onions on it. Place a piece of cod on top then fold bamboo net up. Secure with bamboo skewers.

- Heat oil in a wok over medium heat and deep-fry fish for about 2 minutes. Drain and remove bamboo skewers and net. Repeat with remaining cod and spring onions.

- Place deep-fried spring onion wrapped cod in a preheated oven at 180°C and bake for 10 minutes.

- Slice pickled cucumbers into thin strips and lay on 4 serving plates like a carparccio. Place a spring onion wrapped cod on each plate and serve immediately.

braised whole sea cucumber with sun-dried prawn roe

serves 4 / preparation time: 20 minutes / cooking time: 1 hour

INGREDIENTS

Sun-dried prawn (shrimp) roe	1/2 tsp
Cooking oil	200 ml
Ready-soaked sea cucumber	650 g
Pork belly	200 g, diced
Garlic	10, peeled and chopped
Spring onions (scallions)	5
Basic stock	3 litres (see pg 175)
Ginger	3-cm knob, peeled and chopped
Light soy sauce	75 ml
Dark soy sauce	100 ml
Sugar	110 g
Oyster sauce	1 Tbsp
Shao xing wine	2 Tbsp
Flying fish roe	1 tsp
Wo sun shoots	6 slices, blanched to cook
Quail's eggs	6, hard-boiled and peeled

METHOD

- In a dry non-stick pan, lightly pan-fry sun-dried prawn roe until fragrant. Set aside.

- Heat oil in a wok and lightly fry soaked sea cucumber to firm up its exterior. Drain and set aside.

- Reheat wok and fry pork belly, garlic and spring onions until fragrant. Add basic stock, ginger, soy sauces, sugar, oyster sauce, *shao xing* wine and sea cucumber. Lower heat and simmer for about 1 hour or until pork belly is very soft and tender to the touch.

- Stir in sun-dried prawn roe and fish roe. Thicken sauce with some potato flour solution if desired. Serve immediately with quail eggs and *wo sun* shoots. Garnish with fish roe and spring onion tips as desired.

spicy giant frog legs with pickled chillies

serves 4 / preparation time: 15 minutes / cooking time: 10 minutes

INGREDIENTS

Cooking oil	2 Tbsp
Garlic	2 cloves, peeled and sliced
Ginger	2-cm knob, peeled and minced
Fermented black beans	$^1/_2$ tsp, chopped
Bird's eye chillies	40 g, chopped
Sichuan pickled chillies	20 g (see *chef's note*, pg 127)
Ground chilli paste	2 tsp
Chilli oil	1 Tbsp
Sugar	1 tsp
Salt	$^1/_2$ tsp
Giant frog legs	300 g
Shao xing wine	2 tsp
Potato flour	1 tsp

garnish

Coriander (cilantro) leaves	2 sprigs, chopped
Spring onions (scallions)	2, chopped

METHOD

- Heat cooking oil in a wok and sauté garlic, ginger, fermented black beans and bird's eye chillies until fragrant. Add pickled chillies, chilli paste, chilli oil, sugar and salt. Mix well and remove from heat.
- Wash and pat dry frog legs. Mix with *shao xing* wine, potato flour and stir-fried fermented black beans.
- Steam frog legs for 5–6 minutes until cooked.
- Sprinkle chopped coriander and spring onions over evenly. Serve immediately.

sautéed crab claw and prawns with salted duck egg crust

serves 1 / preparation time: 20 minutes / cooking time: 10 minutes

INGREDIENTS

Green crab claw	1
Live king prawns (shrimps)	2
Salted duck egg yolks	50 g
Potato flour	2 Tbsp
Cooking oil	200 ml
Salted butter	3 tsp
Five spice salt*	$^1/_8$ tsp
Salad greens	

**five spice salt*

Salt	5 Tbsp
Cinnamon bark	2-cm length
Star anise	1
Five spice powder	$^1/_8$ tsp
Sugar	1 tsp
Garlic salt	1 tsp (optional)

METHOD

- Freeze fresh crab claw for about 2 hours and place live king prawns in an ice bath to put them to sleep.
- Meanwhile, prepare five spice salt. Dry-fry salt, cinnamon and star anise in a non-stick pan until light brown in colour. Add five spice powder, sugar and garlic salt (optional). Allow to cool and use as required. Store in an airtight container for up to a few months.
- Crack frozen crab claw using a cleaver, then remove shell. Leave only the tip of the shell intact.
- Peel head and shell off prawns and discard.
- Steam salted duck egg yolks for 5 minutes until cooked. Leave to cool before chopping into tiny bits.
- Coat crab claw and prawns with some potato flour. Heat cooking oil over medium heat and fry crab claw and prawns until cooked. Drain and set aside.
- Heat a wok over low heat and melt butter. Add salted egg yolks and stir until foam starts to form. Add crab claw and prawns and sprinkle five spice salt over evenly. Coat well.
- Arrange crab claw and prawns on a serving plate. Garnish with remaining egg yolk sauce and fresh salad greens. Serve immediately.

from left: spicy giant frog legs with pickled chillies; sautéed crab claw and prawns with salted duck egg crust

yellow croaker fish fillet with egg white in a glutinous rice wine brine

serves 4 / preparation time: 20 minutes / cooking time: 10 minutes

INGREDIENTS

Yellow croaker fish fillet	180 g
Salt	to taste
Sugar	to taste
Black peppercorns	$1/2$ tsp, crushed
Potato flour	1 Tbsp, mixed with some water
Egg white	1
Bamboo shoots	120 g, peeled and cut into 0.3-cm slices
Dried wood ear fungus	20 g, soaked to soften
Cooking oil	1 Tbsp
Ground black pepper	to taste
Basic stock	100 ml (see pg 175)
Rice wine brine	3 tsp (see *chef's note*, pg 50)
Sweet glutinous rice grains	20 g

METHOD

- Marinate fish fillet with salt, sugar, crushed peppercorns and egg white. Chill lightly for about 30 minutes. This will give the fish a firmer and smoother coating when cooked.
- Blanch bamboo shoots and wood ear fungus in hot water separately until cooked. Set aside.
- Heat oil in a wok and stir-fry bamboo shoots. Season with salt and pepper. Set aside.
- In a clean wok, add basic stock, rice wine brine, sweet glutinous rice grains, blanched black fungus and stir-fried bamboo shoots. Lower fish in and simmer until cooked. Season to taste with salt, sugar and pepper then thicken with some potato flour solution.
- Dish out onto a serving plate and serve immediately.

chef's note: Yellow croaker (*huang yu*) is such a popular Shanghainese delicacy that it suffered from over-fishing. Today, most of the yellow croakers found in the market are farmed. Many believe that the taste and texture of the farmed fishes are inferior to those fished from the sea. As such, the price of yellow croakers varies greatly, with those fished from the sea costing up to 20 times more. Be wary of being overcharged when purchasing yellow croakers, as it may be hard to differentiate between the two types of fish.

photograph on pg 75

shanghai fried eel strips
with bean sprouts and freshly grated ginger

serves 4 / preparation time: 20 minutes / cooking time: 10 minutes

INGREDIENTS

Red chilli	1, cut into long strips
Yellow capsicum (bell pepper)	1/6, cut into long strips
Bean sprouts	30 g
Cooking oil	4 Tbsp
Ginger	2-cm knob, peeled and minced
Garlic	10, peeled and minced
Baby yellow eel	200 g, cut into strips
Basic stock	100 ml (see pg 175)
Sugar	1 tsp
Dark soy sauce	2 tsp
Ground white pepper	a dash
Potato flour	2 Tbsp, mixed with some water
Sesame oil	a few drops
Spring onion (scallion)	1, thinly shredded and soaked in ice water

METHOD

● Lightly blanch chilli and capsicum strips in hot water then sauté with bean sprouts. Season with salt to taste. Set aside.

● Heat oil in a wok and add minced ginger and minced garlic. Sauté until fragrant then add eel strips. Add basic stock and season with sugar, dark soy sauce and pepper.

● Lower heat and simmer for about 2 minutes until eel is tender and soft. Thicken mixture with potato flour solution and transfer to a serving plate with sautéed chilli, capsicum and bean sprouts. Drizzle sesame oil over.

● Serve immediately. (If desired, sprinkle some fried garlic on the dish to give it a more robust flavour.) Garnish with spring onion curls.

chef's note: This is a traditional Shanghainese dish that requires the eel to be extremely well cooked until it almost melts in your mouth. For this dish to be successful, it is important that the eel used is live or extremely fresh. Choose baby eels that are not more than 25 cm long, so the meat will be more tender. As handling live eels requires some skill and practice, get the fishmonger to clean it for you.

simmered carp in a vinegar and soy broth

serves 4 / preparation time: 15 minutes / cooking time: 10 minutes

INGREDIENTS

Green capsicum (bell pepper)	$1/6$, cut into thin 5-cm strips
Yellow capsicum bell pepper)	$1/6$, cut into thin 5-cm strips
Red capsicum (bell pepper)	$1/6$, cut into thin 5-cm strips
Dried Chinese mushrooms	2, soaked to soften and cut into thin 5-cm strips
Bamboo shoots	10, small, cut into thin 5-cm strips
Cooking oil	1 tsp
Salt	to taste
Carp	1, about 600 g
Potato flour	2 tsp, mixed with a little water
Zhen jiang vinegar	50 ml

seasoning

Ginger	2-cm knob, peeled and sliced
Salt	$1/4$ tsp
Sugar	5 tsp
Dark soy sauce	$1/2$ tsp
Water	70 ml

METHOD

- Blanch capsicums, mushrooms and bamboo shoots in hot water to cook. Drain well. Lightly stir-fry with oil and salt to taste.

- Pour some water in a wok and bring to the boil. Lower carp in and reduce heat to simmer for about 5 minutes until fish is cooked.

- In the meantime, combine seasoning and bring to the boil. Lightly thicken with potato flour solution then add vinegar.

- Place fish on a serving plate. Ladle vinegar sauce over and garnish with sautéed vegetables. Serve immediately.

chef's note: This method of poaching fish was made popular by chefs from Hangzhou. Simmering the fish makes it very tender and reduces the taste of 'mud', commonly associated with freshwater fish, significantly.

stir-fried hairy crab powder with eggs and sea urchin

serves 6 / preparation time: 20 minutes / cooking time: 10 minutes

INGREDIENTS

Eggs	6
Salt	to taste
Sugar	to taste
Ground white pepper	a dash
Shao xing wine	1 tsp
Shallot oil	2 Tbsp (see pg 43)
Minced ginger	$^1/_2$ tsp
Hairy crabmeat and roe	60 g (see *chef's note*, pg 54)
Sea urchin	30 g

METHOD

- Using an egg cutter, carefully make an opening on top of each egg without damaging shells. Empty contents into a bowl and blanch eggshells in hot water. Peel away layer of thin membrane inside eggshells. Drain eggshells dry.

- Add salt, sugar, pepper and *shao xing* wine to eggs and lightly whisk until well blended.

- Heat shallot oil in a non-stick pan and lightly fry ginger until fragrant. Add eggs and hairy crabmeat and roe and sauté. The mixture will set like scrambled eggs. Spoon into eggshells.

- Top filled eggshells with raw sea urchin. Garnish as desired and serve immediately.

shanghai style steamed freshwater fish

serves 4 / preparation time: 15 minutes / cooking time: 10 minutes

INGREDIENTS

Jinhua ham	80 g
Sugar	to taste
Ground white pepper	a dash
Bamboo shoot	1, peeled and cut into 0.5-cm slices
Shi yu (hilsa herring) fillet	1, about 350 g
Dried Chinese mushrooms	3, soaked to soften, stems discarded
Pigs's caul	1, about 20 x 20-cm
Spring onion (scallion)	1, cut into 5-cm lengths

METHOD

- Blanch ham in boiling water for 3 minutes to remove any impurities. Discard liquid and place ham in a heatproof (flameproof) bowl. Add enough water to cover ham then cover bowl with plastic wrap. Place in a steamer for about 1 hour. Remove ham and slice into 3 equal pieces. Season ham juice to taste with sugar and pepper. Set aside.

- Blanch bamboo shoot slices in hot water for 10 minutes until soft and cooked.

- Make 3 shallow cuts (spaced evenly apart) on one side of fish. Insert a mushroom, bamboo shoot slice and ham into each cut. Wrap fish fillet with pig's caul.

- Place spring onion on fish fillet then place fish fillet and ham juice into a steamer and steam separately for about 10 minutes until fish is cooked. Discard spring onion and place fish on a serving plate. Spoon ham juice over fish and serve immediately.

chef's note: Pig's caul is the lacy membrane around the pig's stomach. If desired, you can marinate the caul with *mei gui lou* Chinese wine for a day to give it a unique wine flavour.

Shi yu (hilsa herring) is a very popular freshwater fish from the Shanghai/ Jiangzhe region. The best time to eat this fish is just after the Lunar New Year month. Many Shanghai gourmets look forward to this time of the year to feast on this delicacy.

Poultry

Chicken features heavily in the cuisine of Shanghai and must be the meat most often presented at the banquet table.

The city's legendary drunken chicken, for one, has captured the tastebuds and imaginations of diners the world over. In the autumn and winter months, chicken is sometimes air-dried, giving it intensified flavours that make it an excellent ingredient for soups and braises. But more commonly, chickens are preferred market-fresh. Each morning, Shanghainese housewives can be spotted inspecting chickens destined for the dinner table that very same day. The prospective chicken's eyes and feathers are checked and it is lifted to get a gauge of its weight. But most importantly, the kind of chicken is chosen based on the sort of dish it will feature in. For soups and stews, older chickens offer more flavour, while the tender flesh of younger birds is ideal for braising and poaching. Cao ji, also referred to as san huang ji, are free-range chickens and are preferred over the farmed rou ji. They are prized for their taste, an even layer of fat under the skin and beautiful yellow hue. Cao ji have firmer flesh and taste distinctly of, well, chicken! Farmed breeds are simply no match for them. When it comes to preparing drunken chicken, only the free-range chickens bought from the markets of Shanghai will do. The fowls have a unique flavour that is delightfully strong and fragrant. They also form the foundation of some of the best chicken consommé I've ever tasted in the course of my entire career! To make tu ji tang (free range chicken soup), all you need is several stalks of spring onions and a tiny piece of smashed ginger placed in a pot of hot water with a cleaned free range chicken. Simply double boil the ingredients for three to four hours. The enticing aroma never fails to draw random visitors into my kitchen.

wok-fried diced chicken
with pickled chillies in spicy sauce

serves 4 / preparation time: 15 minutes / cooking time: 10 minutes

INGREDIENTS

Cooking oil for frying	
Yellow capsicums (bell peppers)	4
Chicken leg	600 g, cut into 2-cm pieces
Garlic	2 cloves, peeled and chopped
Ginger	2-cm knob, peeled and chopped
Spring onions (scallions)	2, cut into 5-cm lengths
Dried chillies	10, soaked to soften
Sichuan pickled chillies	50 g (see *chef's note*, pg 127)
Carrot	$^1/_2$, peeled and sliced

sauce

Black vinegar	50 ml
Chilli sauce	60 ml
Light soy sauce	2 tsp
Oyster sauce	2 tsp
Dark soy sauce	1 Tbsp
Water	50 ml
Sugar	25 g
Shao xing wine	1 Tbsp
Cooking oil	2 Tbsp

METHOD

- Heat some oil for frying over medium heat and lightly fry whole capsicums until surface is cooked. Drain and wipe off excessive oil with absorbent paper. Slice capsicums open at a 45° angle and remove core and seeds. Set aside on a serving dish.

- Blanch chicken pieces in a pot of boiling water until 60% cooked. Drain well.

- Mix all sauce ingredients in a bowl and stir until contents are dissolved.

- In a non-stick pan, sear chicken pieces until surface is lightly browned. Add some cooking oil and sauté garlic, ginger, spring onions and dried and pickled chillies until fragrant.

- Add carrot and sauce and sauté. Ensure sauce is well and evenly absorbed by chicken, so there is little remaining sauce in pan.

- Remove from heat and dish into prepared yellow capsicums. Serve immediately.

crispy duck breast with sweet osmanthus sauce

serves 4 / preparation time: 4 hours / cooking time: 10 minutes

INGREDIENTS

Duck breasts	1 kg, about 4 pieces
Baby bamboo shoots	300 g
Salt	to taste
Cooking oil	500 ml

sauce

Hoisin sauce	4 Tbsp
Water	4 Tbsp
Dried Osmanthus blossoms	2 tsp
Salt	a pinch
Ground white pepper	a pinch
Plum sauce	2 Tbsp

wine marinade

Salt	2 tsp
Mei gui lou wine	2 Tbsp
Ginger	3-cm knob, peeled and finely chopped
Spring onions (scallions)	2, finely chopped
Garlic	2 cloves, peeled and finely chopped
Shallots	3 cloves, peeled and finely chopped
Five spice powder	$1/8$ tsp

vinegar marinade

Maltose	125 g
Water	400 ml
Chinese red vinegar	1 Tbsp
Chinese rice vinegar	100 ml

METHOD

- Combine ingredients for wine marinade and rub all over duck breasts. Leave refrigerated for about 4 hours.

- Briefly blanch marinated duck breasts in hot water until skins contract. Drain well.

- In another pot, melt maltose with water over low heat. Add red vinegar and rice vinegar and bring to the boil. Place duck breasts in a sieve over pot and ladle vinegar marinade repeatedly over. Ensure duck skin is evenly coated.

- Use hanging hooks or a long barbecue skewer to skewer duck breasts and hang them up. Ensure that duck breasts do not touch each other. Use an electric fan to blow duck breasts for about 3 hours 30 minutes to 4 hours until duck skin is completely dry to the touch.

- Meanwhile, prepare sauce. Mix hoisin sauce with water. Add 1 tsp Osmanthus blossoms and simmer sauce for 3 minutes to release flavours. Add salt and pepper to adjust taste if desired. In another bowl, add remaining Osmanthus blossoms to plum sauce and steam for 15 minutes to release flavours. Combine with hoisin sauce mixture. Set aside.

- Bring a pot of water to the boil then blanch baby bamboo shoots until cooked. Season to taste with salt and transfer to serving plates.

- When skin of duck breasts is dry to the touch, heat cooking oil in a wok and fry over low heat for about 6 minutes. Turn duck breasts over frequently as they are frying to ensure duck cooks to an even, deep golden brown colour. Drain on absorbent paper.

- Slice duck into serving slices and arrange on prepared serving plates. Serve immediately with sauce either as a topping or as a dip. Garnish with dried Osmanthus blossoms if desired.

pan-seared foie gras
with spring bamboo shoots and quail's eggs

serves 4 / preparation time: 15 minutes / cooking time: 20 minutes

INGREDIENTS

Foie gras	200 g
Olive oil	2 tsp
Sesame oil	1 tsp
Black peppercorns	$1/4$ tsp, crushed
Coriander (cilantro) stem	1, minced
Garlic	1 clove, peeled and minced
Shallot	1, peeled and minced
Salt	to taste
Bamboo shoots	300 g, peeled and cut into 0.5-cm slices
Cooking oil	1 tsp
Quail's eggs	4

METHOD

- Lightly chill foie gras and use your hands to separate the two lobes. Using a sharp knife, trim away any connective membranes, veins or green bile. Cut into slices each about 1-cm thick. Rinse and pat dry.

- Combine olive oil, sesame oil, half the black pepper, minced coriander, garlic and shallot with a little salt and marinate foie gras for 10 minutes in the refrigerator before use.

- Place bamboo shoots into boiling water for about 15 minutes until cooked. Drain and pat dry. Season to taste with salt and remaining black pepper.

- Heat cooking oil in a non-stick pan and sauté bamboo shoots. Transfer to serving plates.

- In another pan, fry quail's eggs individually, sunny side up. Arrange on prepared serving plates.

- Pan-sear marinated foie gras to desired doneness. Arrange on serving plates and serve immediately.

stir-fried minced pigeon with fragrant pear in crispy wrappers

serves 4 / preparation time: 30 minutes / cooking time: 15 minutes

INGREDIENTS

Phyllo pastry	8 sheets
Green chives	8 stalks, blanched and pat dry
Fragrant pear	1, cut into 8 round slices and cored

filling

Cooking oil	2 Tbsp
Pigeon meat	300 g, cut into 0.5-cm cubes
Bamboo shoots	50 g, cut into 0.5-cm cubes
Water chestnuts	50 g, peeled and cut into 0.5-cm cubes
Local celery	50 g, cut into 0.5-cm cubes
Shiitake mushrooms	50 g, cut into 0.5-cm cubes
Yellow chives	3 stalks, cut into 0.5-cm pieces
Garlic	1 clove, peeled and minced
Coriander (cilantro) stems	2, minced
Shallot	1 clove, peeled and minced

seasoning

Hoisin sauce	2 tsp
Dark soy sauce	1 tsp
Light soy sauce	to taste
Oyster oil	to taste
Ground white pepper	a dash
Shao xing wine	1 tsp
Sesame oil	1/2 tsp

METHOD

- Prepare filling. Heat cooking oil in a non-stick pan and sauté pigeon and bamboo shoots until half-cooked. Add all other ingredients and seasoning. Add 2 Tbsp water to make dish moist if necessary. Divide filling into 8 equal portions.

- Lay a phyllo pastry sheet out and spoon a portion of filling on. Bring edges of phyllo pastry up to look like a money pouch. Secure with a stalk of blanched green chive. Repeat to make 7 more parcels.

- Preheat oven to 180°C and bake pigeon parcels until crisp and light golden brown in colour.

- Make a cut on each slice of pear and fit one around each pigeon parcel. Serve immediately.

crispy pigeon with sichuan peppercorns, vinegar and spring onion toppings

serves 4 / preparation time: 4 hours / cooking time: 15 minutes

INGREDIENTS

Pigeons	4, each about 400 g
Five spice salt	6 tsp (see pg 73)
Shallots	8 cloves, peeled and finely chopped
Spring onions (scallions)	4, finely chopped
Garlic	16 cloves, peeled and 8 finely chopped
Young ginger	100 g, peeled and finely chopped
Maltose	125 g
Water	400 ml
Chinese red vinegar	1 Tbsp
Chinese rice vinegar	100 ml

sauce

Peanut oil	200 ml
Mei gui lou wine	4 tsp
Salt	50 g
Sugar	25 g
Light soy sauce	4 tsp
Chilli powder	20 g
Curry powder	20 g
Sesame oil	2 Tbsp
Chilli oil	50 ml
Black vinegar	2 Tbsp
Crisp-fried shallots	200 g

METHOD

- Marinate cavity of pigeons evenly with five spice salt. Combine shallots, spring onions, finely chopped garlic and ginger and place into cavity of pigeons. Seal opening of pigeons with bamboo skewers.

- In a deep pot, bring some water to the boil and briefly blanch pigeons until skin contracts. Drain well.

- In another pot, melt maltose with water over low heat. Add red vinegar and rice vinegar and bring to the boil. Dip drained pigeons in and ladle marinade over to ensure that pigeons are well and evenly coated.

- Use hanging hooks or a long barbecue skewer to hang pigeons up. Ensure that pigeons are not touching. Use an electric fan to blow-dry pigeons for about 3 hours 30 minutes to 4 hours until skin is completely dry to the touch.

- Meanwhile, chop remaining garlic finely. Heat peanut oil in a non-stick pan and fry garlic until light golden brown in colour. Turn off heat and add in remaining sauce ingredients, with vinegar and crisp-fried shallots at the last. Set aside.

- When skin of pigeons are dry to the touch, heat some cooking oil in a wok and fry pigeons over low heat for about 15 minutes. Turn pigeons over frequently as they are frying to ensure pigeons cook to an even, deep golden brown colour.

- Drain on absorbent paper and serve immediately with sauce either as a topping or as a dip.

slow-cooked duck breast
with sun-dried pork and bean curd

serves 4 / preparation time: 15 minutes / cooking time: 2 hours

INGREDIENTS

Mature duck	1, about 2 kg
Air-dried salted pork	100 g, cut into small pieces
Fresh pork belly	300 g, cut into small pieces
Pickled bamboo shoots	300 g, cut into small pieces
Water	5 litres
Spring onions (scallions)	2, lightly bruised
Ginger	2-cm knob, peeled and finely chopped
Bai ye bean curd sheets	a few, tied into 20 knots

seasoning

Shao xing wine	2 Tbsp
Salt	to taste
Ground white pepper	a dash
Sugar	to taste

METHOD

- Cut duck breast out and set aside. Cut remaining duck into large pieces.

- Blanch air-dried pork, pork belly and pickled bamboo shoots in hot water to remove any impurities. Drain and set aside.

- Bring 5 litres water to the boil. Add all ingredients except bean curd knots and seasoning and return to the boil over medium heat for about 1 hour to fully release flavours. Lower heat and add bean curd knots. Slow-cook until ingredients are soft and stock is rich.

- Remove duck breast and air-dried salted pork from pot. Cut into serving sizes and divide equally among 4 serving dishes.

- Return stock to the boil and add seasoning to taste. Ladle over duck and pork. Serve immediately.

Meat

When the Chinese say 'meat', they invariably mean 'pork', a key ingredient in Shanghai and Chinese cookery.

While alternative meats have been introduced to and served at the plentiful Shanghainese table, none have surpassed the popularity of pork. And the chefs of Shanghai have devised a plethora of mouth-watering dishes that celebrate the gastronomic delights of every inch of the pig. No part of the animal goes to waste. Simply savour *dong bo rou* (red braised pork belly), *hong shao yuan ti* (braised pork knuckles), *shi zi tou* ('lion's head' dumplings) and *yan du xian* (air-dried pork and bamboo shoot soup) as proof! And by bringing together deceptively ordinary ingredients, they've created scrumptious regional specialities. The lynchpin of their fabulous *xiao long bao* (juicy pork dumplings), the ingredient that gives it that velvety rich, meaty explosion in your mouth, is the discreet inclusion of pork skin.

To fully appreciate the Shanghainese's mastery over pork dishes requires an understanding of their unique brand of braising, often with soy sauce. It is a method that first calls for sugar to be caramelised in oil before the main ingredients are added. It is this caramelised sugar, combined with red yeast rice and dark soy that give Shanghainese braised meats their glorious sheen and subtle reddish hue. After spring onions, Shanghai's light and dark soy sauces, and Chinese wine are added to the pan, the dish is simmered over a low fire until the meat is achingly tender and the sauce is reduced to a gravy-like consistency. Due to the amount of sugar used in the dish, the reduced sauce is so thick that it doesn't even need to be thickened with flour or starch. The resulting flavours are sweet and intense. It is this style of preparing pork, in particular, that distinguishes the Shanghainese as masters of braising.

shanghainese red braised pork knuckles

serves 4 / preparation time: 30 minutes / cooking time: 3 hours

INGREDIENTS

Pork front knuckle	I
Cooking oil	250 ml
Sugar	50g
Rock sugar	80 g
Ginger	3-cm knob, peeled
Spring onions (scallions)	20 g
Water	2 litres
Spinach leaves	150 g

seasoning

Shao xing wine	3 Tbsp
Oyster sauce	2 Tbsp
Dark soy sauce	30 ml
Light soy sauce	30 ml
Red yeast powder	I tsp
Salt	$\frac{1}{2}$ tsp

METHOD

- Blanch pork knuckle in hot water for 10 minutes then drain and remove any remaining hair attached on skin.

- Heat oil in a wok until warm and melt sugar and rock sugar to get a caramelised solution. Add pork knuckle, ginger and spring onions and lightly fry until fragrant.

- Add in seasoning and water. Bring to the boil for about 15 minutes to fully release flavours. Turn down heat and simmer for about 3 hours or until pork knuckle is tender to the touch of a fork.

- Lightly blanch spinach leaves then drain and wrap leaves into round dumpling shapes using plastic wrap. Remove plastic wrap and arrange spinach balls on a serving plate.

- Transfer pork knuckle to the plate. Reheat sauce and ladle over spinach and pork knuckle. Serve immediately. (If a thicker gravy is desired, thicken sauce with a little potato or corn flour solution.)

'lion's head' hairy crab and meat dumplings in broth

serves 4 / preparation time: 30 minutes / cooking time: 30 minutes

INGREDIENTS

Cooking oil	50 ml
Ginger	2-cm knob, peeled and minced
Hairy crabmeat and roe	100 g (see *chef's note*, pg 54)
Basic stock	1 litre (see pg 175)
Salt	to taste
Ground white powder	a dash
Potato flour	2 tsp, mixed with some water
Minced pork belly	200 g, chilled
Shao xing wine	2 tsp
Light soy sauce	1 tsp
Ginger wine solution	4 Tbsp (see *chef's note*)
Chinese baby cabbage	4
Winter melon rings	4, each about 50 g
Chinese flowering cabbage (*cai xin*)	4 stalks, blanched (optional)

METHOD

- Heat oil in a wok and sauté minced ginger until fragrant. Add hairy crabmeat and roe with 2 Tbsp basic stock then season with salt and pepper. Thicken with potato flour solution. Set aside.

- Place minced pork belly in a bowl. The meat must be properly chilled when using. Add *shao xing* wine and keep stirring in one direction until meat binds together. Gradually add light soy sauce and ginger wine solution. Form mixture into 4 round balls and chill for 2 hours to allow flavours to be fully absorbed.

- Bring remaining basic stock to the boil and carefully simmer meat balls for 30 minutes over low heat. Add Chinese cabbage after 15 minutes. Remove meat balls and leave to cool for a few minutes.

- Scoop tops off meat balls and fill with hairy crab mixture.

- Place meat balls onto winter melon rings with the hairy crab mixture facing up. Steam for 10 minutes to reheat. Serve with juices and a stalk of Chinese flowering cabbage if desired.

chef's note: Ginger wine solution is a mixture of ginger juice (20%), *shao xing* wine (20%) and water (60%). It is usually used to increase the aroma of cooked dishes. The minced pork belly should be 60% lean meat and 40% fatty meat. This makes for a much smoother and moist dumpling.

slow-cooked candied chinese ham with lotus seeds

serves 4 / preparation time: 15 minutes / cooking time: 40 minutes

INGREDIENTS

Jinhua ham (30% fat, 60% lean meat)	300 g, chilled
Sugar	100 g
Honey	100 g
Salted Osmanthus blossoms	2 tsp
Fresh lotus seeds	200 g
Water	5 Tbsp
Chinese lotus buns	20

METHOD

- Using a sharp knife, cut chilled ham into thin slices, each about 0.2-cm thick.

- In a deep heatproof (flameproof) bowl, lay the sliced ham neatly to cover the bottom surface of the bowl.

- Combine sugar, honey and salted Osmanthus blossoms with fresh lotus seeds and pour into bowl. Add water and steam for 40 minutes until sugar has dissolved and ham has absorbed the flavours.

- Carefully pour any juices from steaming into another container, using a plate to cover the deep bowl to prevent the ingredients from falling out.

- Overturn the bowl onto a plate to unmould the ham. Arrange some cooked lotus seeds around the candied ham and pour juices over evenly. Serve immediately with steamed Chinese lotus buns.

chef's note: Many Chinese specialty stores will have ready-cooked Jinhua ham for sale, so there is no need to prepare it yourself. But for those who prefer to, steam the ham for about 3 hours then discard the steaming liquid. Cover the ham with a clean kitchen towel and place a heavy object on it for about 30 minutes to firm it up. Wrap with cling wrap and refrigerate until ready to use.

Chinese Lotus buns are commonly available in Chinese supermarkets. If unavailable, use, thickly sliced steamed Chinese buns (*mantou*).

slow-cooked pork marrow and beef tendon with turnip

serves 4 / preparation time: 15 minutes / cooking time: 1 hour 30 minutes

INGREDIENTS

White turnip	400 g
Beef tendon	300 g
Pork marrow shanks	4
Cooking oil	5 Tbsp
Ginger	5-cm knob, peeled and sliced
Spring onions (scallions)	5
Water	4 litres
Watercress	500 g
Potato flour	1 Tbsp, mixed with some water (optional)

seasoning

Dark soy sauce	2 Tbsp
Oyster sauce	to taste
Fermented soy bean paste	5 Tbsp
Sugar	to taste
Shao xing wine	5 Tbsp

METHOD

- Peel white turnip and cut to get 8 rounds, each about 3.5-cm thick. Chop remaining turnip into large chunks.

- Bring a pot of water to the boil and blanch beef tendon and pork marrow shanks for 2 minutes to remove any impurities. Drain and discard liquid.

- Heat oil in a large wok and sauté ginger and spring onions until fragrant. Add beef tendon and pork marrow shanks. Pour in water and add seasoning. Bring to the boil then lower heat and slow-cook for about 1 hour 30 minutes or until beef tendon is soft to the touch of a fork. In the last 15 minutes of cooking, add turnip and cook until soft.

- Remove 8 turnip rounds and cut a hole in the middle of each round. Cut braised beef tendon with a pair of scissors into bite-size pieces and place into holes.

- Sauté watercress with a little oil, water and salt.

- Arrange pork marrow shanks, turnip rounds and watercress on a serving plate. Heat sauce and thicken with potato flour solution if desired. Pour over dish and serve immediately.

the legendary *dong po* braised pork

serves 4 / preparation time: 20 minutes / cooking time: 2 hours

INGREDIENTS

Pork belly	300 g
Cooking oil	100 ml
Spring onions (scallions)	2, lightly bruised and 2 cut into 2-cm lengths
Ginger	2-cm knob, peeled and finely chopped
Water	1 litre
Salt	to taste
Potato flour	2 Tbsp, mixed with some water

seasoning

Sugar	2 Tbsp
Oyster sauce	1 Tbsp
Dark soy sauce	1 Tbsp
Light soy sauce	1 Tbsp
Rock sugar	50 g
Shao xing wine	3 Tbsp

METHOD

- Blanch pork belly in hot water for 5 minutes to remove any impurities. Drain and set aside.

- Heat oil in a wok and stir-fry lightly bruised spring onion and ginger until fragrant. Add water and seasoning then bring to the boil. Lower heat and simmer pork belly for about 2 hours until it is very tender and soft to the touch of a fork. Drain meat and reserve gravy.

- Chill meat, then carefully cut it into long strips. (Cutting the meat when it is very hot will cause it to fall apart.) Using the odd-shaped pieces of cut meat, build up a pyramid then and carefully place the pork strips over to cover. Reheat pork pyramid with some reserved gravy.

- Heat 1 Tbsp oil and lightly sauté spring onion lengths with a little water and salt. Arrange around pork pyramid.

- Thicken remaining gravy with potato flour solution, pour over meat and serve immediately.

sugar cane and tea-smoked pork ribs

serves 4 / preparation time: 15 minutes / cooking time: 1 hour

INGREDIENTS

Pork spare ribs	600 g
Cooking oil	250 ml
Ginger	5-cm knob, peeled and shredded
Spring onions (scallions)	3
Water	500 ml
Shao xing wine	1 Tbsp
Salt	to taste
Red glutinous rice wine yeast	50 ml
Tomato sauce	5 Tbsp
Sugar	150 g

for smoking

Aluminium foil	30 x 30-cm sheet
Plain (all-purpose) flour	5 Tbsp
Tea leaves	1 Tbsp, soaked
Sugar cane	5 sticks, each 5-cm, lightly smashed

METHOD

- Cut pork ribs into 8-cm lengths. Deep-fry in hot oil until light golden brown. Drain and set aside.

- In the same oil, deep-fry half the ginger shreds until light golden brown. Pat dry with paper towels and reserve for garnish.

- In the same oil, sauté spring onions and remaining ginger until fragrant. Add water, *shao xing* wine, salt, red glutinous rice wine yeast, tomato sauce and 50 g sugar. Bring to the boil and add spare ribs. Lower heat to medium and simmer ribs for about 1 hour until soft to the touch. Remove ribs and strain sauce.

- Arrange cooked ribs evenly on a wire rack.

- Line a dry wok with aluminium foil and add flour, tea leaves, sugar cane and remaining sugar. Mix well and sprinkle some water over mixture. Cover wok and cook over high heat until yellow smoke appears.

- Place wire rack of ribs in. Cover and smoke for about 2 minutes. Remove to a serving plate.

- Reheat sauce and pour over smoked ribs, Garnish with fried ginger shreds and serve immediately.

chef's note: Red glutinous rice wine yeast (*hong jiu zhao*) is the residue leftover from the making of glutinous rice wine. It is mixed with red yeast rice and further fermented, then steamed and dried to create a mixture that gives a unique flavour to dishes.

Vegetables and Bean Curd

The abundance and variety of vegetables in Shanghai has to be seen to be believed.

The distinct seasons the city enjoys also means that at different times of the year, a scrumptiously different harvest of nature's bounty is brought to the table to be savoured.

Summertime brings sweet, perfumed melons and fruit. Succulent winter melons make excellent soups at this time of year and are the perfect addition to braised dishes as they absorb the flavours of the other ingredients they're cooked with. Hairy melons are showcased to their best advantage when paired with giant frog legs, a little bean paste and some fresh chilli for added zing of spice. In the winter, green leafy vegetables come to the fore. Kale, Chinese flowering cabbage, spinach and many other vegetables are simply much more flavourful, boasting a natural sweetness, at this time of year. Unique to Shanghai are vegetables like *chao tou* (grass head vegetable), which grows in abundance in Shanghai. It tastes like grass, thus the name, and is best served quickly sautéed because the delicate sprouts lose their colour quickly in the heat. *Ta cai* (pagoda vegetable) found only in winter, has a close circular thatch of dark green leaves with white stems. When stacked one atop the other at market stalls, they look like teetering pagodas. *Ji cai* (shepherd's purse), available all year round, is usually preserved and canned. When used fresh, it is served with soups, crabmeat or bean curd.

ji cai and bean curd sheet rolled with pine nuts and salted vegetables

serves 4 / preparation time: 30 minutes / cooking time: 10 minutes

INGREDIENTS

Ji cai	1.5 kg
Pickled mustard	100 g
Pine nuts	50 g, roasted
Salt	to taste
Sugar	to taste
Sesame oil	$^1/_2$ Tbsp
Basic stock	200 ml (see pg 175)
Bai ye bean curd sheets	5 sheets, each about 30 x 30 cm
Cooking oil	
Sweet peas	8 pods
Yellow cherry tomatoes	8, cut into small pieces
Red cherry tomatoes	8, cut into small pieces
Hon shimeji mushrooms	16

METHOD

- Remove hard stem from *ji cai* and blanch in hot water for about 2 minutes until cooked. Drain and place in an ice bath for a few minutes to cool it down and help it retain its green colour. Drain and cut into very fine sheds.

- Wash and blanch pickled mustard to reduce its saltiness. Cut into small 0.5-cm **cubes**.

- Combine *ji cai*, roasted pine nuts and pickled mustard and season to taste with salt, sugar and sesame oil.

- Bring basic stock to the boil then remove from heat. Soak *bai ye* sheets in hot stock briefly to soften. Drain and lay flat on a working surface. Spoon *ji cai* mixture equally onto each *bai ye* sheet and roll each one up. Steam rolls for 8 minutes. Allow to cool before cutting and placing on a serving plate.

- Blanch sweet peas lightly in hot water with a little salt and oil then cut into small pieces.

- Sauté mushrooms lightly with some oil, salt and water.

- Arrange cut *bai ye* rolls with sweet peas, mushrooms and tomatoes. Serve immediately.

shanghai's traditional *kou shan si*

serves 2 / preparation time: 30 minutes / cooking time: 45 minutes

INGREDIENTS

Cooked Jinhua ham (lean)	50 g
Chicken breast	50 g
Bamboo shoots	50 g
Dried Chinese mushrooms	2
Water	500 ml
Vegetable shortening	1 Tbsp
Sweet pea sprouts	80 g
Salt	to taste
Sugar	to taste
Shao xing wine	1 tsp
Potato flour	2 tsp, mixed with some water

METHOD

- Blanch ham, chicken breast, bamboo shoots and mushrooms in hot water for 3 minutes. Discard liquid.

- Bring water to the boil and place blanched ingredients in. Lower heat and simmer for 30 minutes until ingredients are well cooked and flavours are fully released. Remove ingredients and leave to cool. Reserve liquid.

- When ingredients are cool enough to handle, cut them into thin strips about 5-cm long. Keep strips as uniform as possible.

- Apply a layer of vegetable shortening on the inside of 2 deep, round moulds (*kou shan si* moulds). Place a mushroom with its cap facing the bottom of the mould in each mould, then line up shredded chicken, Chinese ham and bamboo shoots along the sides of moulds.

- Wrap moulds up with plastic wrap and steam.

- In the meantime, blanch sweet pea sprouts and press into cavity of moulds. Unmould ingredients onto serving plates.

- Reheat reserved liquid and season to taste with salt, sugar and *shao xing* wine. Add potato flour solution to give it more consistency. Spoon over ingredients and serve immediately.

chef's note: As Jinhua ham is very salty and hard before cooking, buy the cooked variety and choose the lean portions.

mineral bean curd dumplings with hairy crab powder

serves 4 / preparation time: 30 minutes / cooking time: 25 minutes

INGREDIENTS

Unsweetened fresh soy bean milk	1 litre
Spinach leaves	100 g
Squid ink	a few drops
Glucono delta lactone (GDL)	$^1/_2$ tsp
Jinhua ham	50 g, cooked and minced
Cooking oil	1 Tbsp
Ginger	1-cm knob, peeled and minced
Basic stock	2 Tbsp (see pg 175)
Hairy crabmeat and roe	150 g
Salt	to taste
Sugar	to taste
Shao xing wine	1 tsp
Ground white pepper	a dash

METHOD

- Divide soy bean milk equally into 3 portions. Blend (process) 1 portion with spinach leaves using a blender then strain liquid. Add a few drops of squid ink to another portion and mix. Leave 1 portion plain.

- Bring all 3 soy bean milk portions to the boil in separate pots.

- Divide GDL equally into 3 containers. Pour a portion of soy bean milk into each container, starting from near the mouth of the container then pulling back to pour from a greater height. This is to froth and mix the soy bean milk and GDL. Allow the mixtures to cool without stirring the mixtures further. They will set into bean curd once cooled.

- Refrigerate cooled bean curd for 15 minutes then scoop into balls using a melon baller.

- Place bean curd balls and minced ham in a steamer to heat through.

- Prepare hairy crab powder. Heat some oil in a wok and stir-fry minced ginger until fragrant. Add basic stock, hairy crabmeat and roe. Season to taste with salt, sugar, *shao xing* wine and pepper. Pour onto a deep serving plate.

- Arrange 3 coloured bean curd balls and minced ham on the serving plate and serve immediately.

vegetables and bean curd

125

crispy monkey head mushrooms with spicy pickled chillies

serves 4 / preparation time: 20 minutes / cooking time: 10 minutes

INGREDIENTS

Monkey head mushrooms	150 g, soaked and drained
Ginger wine solution	2 Tbsp (see *chef's note*, pg 106)
Egg white	1
Salt	to taste
Sugar	to taste
Cooking oil	250 ml
Garlic	2 cloves, peeled and sliced
Ginger	2-cm knob, peeled and sliced
Fermented black beans	1 tsp, chopped
Water	50 ml
Bird's eye chillies	5
Potato flour	3 Tbsp
Sichuan pickled chillies	50 g, (see *chef's note*)
Endive salad	100 g

METHOD

- Cut mushrooms into 0.5-cm thick slices. Marinate in a mixture of ginger wine solution, egg white, salt and sugar. Mixed evenly.

- Heat 100 ml oil in a wok and sauté sliced garlic and ginger until fragrant. Add chopped fermented black beans and sauté. Add water, bird's eye chillies and salt and sugar to taste. Set aside.

- Coat marinated mushroom slices evenly with potato flour. Heat remaining oil in a wok over medium heat and fry mushrooms until crisp. Remove mushrooms and drain oil.

- Without washing the wok, reheat wok and add pickled chillies. When hot, add fried mushrooms and mix well.

- Arrange endive salad on a serving plate and place fried mushrooms over. Serve immediately.

chef's note: Pickled chillies is a specialty of Sichuan that has found its way onto the dining tables of many Shanghai restaurants in recent years. Small red chillies are marinated in a sweet and sour vinegar solution with herbs, giving the chillies more flavour.

ningbo style slow-cooked baby white cabbage

serves 2 / preparation time: 10 minutes / cooking time: 45 minutes

INGREDIENTS

Cooking oil	50 ml
Pork belly	100 g, thinly sliced
Shao xing wine	2 tsp
Basic stock	500 ml (see pg 175)
Bird's eye chillies	2, lightly slit all over
Rock sugar	1 Tbsp
Light soy sauce	30 ml
Baby white cabbage (*bai cai*)	16 stalks
Sesame oil	a dash
Potato flour	2 tsp, mixed with some water
Salt	to taste

METHOD

- Heat some oil in a wok and stir-fry pork belly until lightly brown and fragrant. Sprinkle in *shao xing* wine and pour in basic stock. Add chillies and season with rock sugar and light soy sauce. Simmer over medium heat until sauce thickens. Add half the baby cabbage and slow cook until cabbage is soft. Sprinkle in sesame oil and dish out onto a serving plate.

- Heat some oil in another wok and sauté remaining baby cabbage. When cabbage is almost ready, add potato flour solution to give cabbage a shinier appearance. Season to taste with salt.

- Arrange sautéed baby cabbage on the serving plate with the slow-cooked cabbage. Garnish with chillies if desired. Serve immediately.

rainbow seasonal vegetables with *wo sun* shoot

serves 4 / preparation time: 20 minutes / cooking time: 15 minutes

INGREDIENTS

Wo sun shoot	1, about 500 g
Salt	to taste
Sugar	to taste
Dried Chinese mushrooms	3, soaked to soften and cut into 6-cm lengths
Carrot	1, peeled and cut into 6-cm lengths
Bamboo shoot	1, cut into 6-cm lengths
Kale	6 stalks, cut into 6-cm lengths
Celery	1 stalk, cut into 6-cm lengths
Basic stock	150 ml (see pg 175)
Sesame oil	1 tsp
Potato flour	2 tsp, mixed with some water

METHOD

- Peel and discard skin and leaves of *wo sun* shoot. Cut stem into 6 rounds, each about 2-cm thick. Use a 4-cm round cutter to cut them into even shapes then use a 2-cm round cutter to cut a hole in the centre of each *wo sun* piece.

- Bring a pot of water to the boil and add salt and sugar. Blanch mushrooms, carrot, bamboo shoot, kale and celery for about 5 minutes until cooked. Drain and allow ingredients to cool down a little.

- When ingredients are cool enough to handle, insert one each of the vegetables and mushroom into the hole of *wo sun* rounds.

- Bring basic stock to the boil and season to taste with salt, sugar and sesame oil. Add *wo sun* parcels in to briefly reheat then add potato flour solution to thicken sauce.

- Arrange *wo sun* parcels on a plate and pour sauce over. Serve immediately.

braised *wa wa* cabbage in *huang men* consommé

serves 6 / preparation time: 20 minutes / cooking time: 2 hours

INGREDIENTS

Wa wa cabbage	1 kg
Salt	to taste
Sugar	to taste
Shao xing wine	2 tsp
Potato flour	1 Tbsp, mixed with some water (optional)

huang men consommé

Stewing hen	1 kg
Pork knuckles	450 g
Chicken feet	300 g
Duck	300 g
Water	3.5 litres
Chinese wolfberries	10
White peppercorns	10
Dried scallops	10 g
Spring onions (scallions)	5
Ginger	5-cm knob
Carrot	100 g, peeled and chopped

METHOD

- Prepare *huang men* consommé. Blanch stewing hen, pork knuckles, chicken feet and duck in hot water for 3 minutes to remove any impurities. Drain and discard water.

- Pour 3.5 litres water into a deep pot and add blanched ingredients and remaining consommé ingredients except carrot. Cook over medium heat for 1 hour 30 minutes.

- Blend (process) carrot with 50 ml of consommé and add to consommé. Cook consommé for a further 30 minutes then strain and discard ingredients except for Chinese wolfberries. Reserve consommé. (This should yield about 2 litres *huang men* consommé. Any excess can be kept refrigerated for up to 5 days.)

- Cut off and discard stems of cabbage. Blanch in hot water over medium heat for about 10 minutes until cabbage is soft and tender to the touch. Drain and pat dry. Set aside.

- Reheat 250 ml *huang men* consommé and season to taste with salt, sugar and *shao xing* wine. Add cabbage and simmer for another 2 minutes to allow flavours to be absorbed.

- Add potato flour solution for better consistency if desired. Serve cabbage and consommé, garnished with Chinese wolfberries. Serve immediately.

chef's note: Huang men consommé is one of the most famous stocks of Yangzhou cuisine. It is known as the supreme consommé in *tan jia cai* (governor Tam's family cuisine), and only the rich and privileged could drink it in the olden days. However, due to the complexity of the recipe and the time consuming cooking technique, it is seldom served today. This is a simplified version of the recipe and although it still feels like a lot of work for a vegetable dish, the taste is definitely worth the effort.

Rice and Noodles

When it comes to breakfast and the starchy,
carbohydrate components of a meal, the taste preferences
in Shanghai are closer to those of Northern China.

Noodles, *mantou* (buns), *bao zi* (meat buns), *you tiao* (fried dough sticks) and soy milk rather than dim sum are eaten for breakfast. At lunchtime, hungry taxi drivers will gather along the crowded streets of popular noodle house enclaves such as Sinan Lu, eager for a quick bite. What hits the spot for them, and most Shanghainese, is a steaming hot bowl of *la mian*, wheat flour noodles that are hand-pulled on the spot. It's not uncommon to find lines of people patiently waiting as the noodle dough is slapped, with a loud thwack, against the countertop then kneaded and stretched. Other variations include *mao er duo* (cat's ear shaped noodles) and *dao xiao mian* (knife-shaved noodles), but *la mian* remains the most popular. The noodles themselves are served in innumerable styles. Find them swimming in delicate roasted eel and fish bone stock, robust pork bone soup or slathered in a heady, spicy sauce called *ba bao la jiang mian*—eight treasure spicy sauce noodles. Each reveals a different facet of the wonderful and complex flavours of Shanghai's noodles.

While noodles are generally considered one-dish meals, rice is always eaten with other dishes. The rice served in Shanghai is short-grained, quite unlike its fragrant, long-grained Thai counterpart. Shanghainese rice dishes, in stark contrast to more familiar Chinese versions of fried rice, are simple. *Cai fan* consists of steamed rice and chopped, blanched vegetables and *xian rou* (salted pork) mixed by hand. But the unusual *nian gao* (Shanghainese rice cakes) are beautiful. When cooked (often with crab or cabbage and shredded pork), the hard discs become so soft that they melt in your mouth.

mung bean noodles with hairy crab roe and green crab claw

serves 1 / preparation time: 20 minutes / cooking time: 10 minutes

INGREDIENTS

Green crab claw	1, about 180 g
Basic stock	250 ml (see pg 175)
Tianjin green pea starch sheets	80 g
Cooking oil	1 Tbsp
Ginger	1-cm knob, peeled and minced
Bean sprouts	a handful
Potato flour	1 Tbsp, mixed with some water
Hairy crab roe	2 Tbsp
Egg white	1

seasoning

Salt	to taste
Sugar	to taste
Ground white pepper	a dash

METHOD

- Place crab claw in the freezer for about 2 hours. Remove and tap claw with a cleaver to break shell. Peel shell off, leaving only a tip of the shell intact. Poach in basic stock until cooked. Remove claw and reserve stock.

- Soak green pea starch sheets in cold water for 5 minutes until soft enough to handle then chop into serving sizes. Blanch until translucent and cooked. Drain and rinse under running water to prevent sticking. Set aside.

- Heat oil in a wok and sauté minced ginger until fragrant. Add reserved stock and seasoning then pea starch sheets and bean sprouts. Thicken with potato flour solution then mix in crab roe and egg white. Do not overcook.

- Serve in martini glasses or as desired and serve immediately.

chef's note: Both hairy crab and green crab roe are used in this recipe. This is because the claws of the hairy crab are small and not very meaty, but its roe lends a unique richness to the bland green pea starch sheets. Green crab claws are used because they are bigger and meatier, and also easily available in China. If green crab claws are not available, use your preferred big, meaty crab claw.

pan-fried egg noodles timbale
with red braised pork and vegetables

serves 1 / preparation time: 30 minutes / cooking time: 15 minutes

INGREDIENTS

Dong bo braised pork	100 g (see pg 113)
Braised pork gravy	200 ml (see pg 113)
Egg noodles	150 g
Egg yolks	3, beaten
Cooking oil	3 Tbsp
Egg whites	3, seasoned with salt to taste
Potato flour	2 tsp, mixed with some water (optional)
Kale	4 stalks, blanched

METHOD

- Lightly chill braised pork before slicing it into long strips about 0.3-cm wide. Spoon some braised pork gravy over meat and steam for 3 minutes to warm it up.

- Blanch egg noodles in hot water until cooked. Lightly rinse with tap water to prevent noodles from sticking.

- Place round or rectangular cake moulds on a baking tray and place noodles in, up to 1 cm high. Bake in a preheated oven at 180°C for 3 minutes until noodles hold their shape. Remove from moulds.

- Place moulded noodles onto a non-stick pan and pour beaten egg yolks evenly over. Pan-fry until crispy. Add oil as necessary. Place cooked noodles on absorbent paper to drain excessive oil.

- Using the same pan, scramble egg whites. Set aside.

- Reheat remaining braised pork gravy and thicken with a little potato flour solution if necessary.

- Place a layer of braised pork on a serving plate and layer with noodles and pork to form a timbale. Arrange scrambled egg white and kale on the side. Pour braised pork gravy over and serve immediately.

chef's note: I was inspired to find a different way to serve *dong bo* pork after seeing it being served as large fatty pork cubes in a number of different restaurants in Shanghai. I combined it with pan-fried noodles or *shuang mian huang* (literally "double side yellow"), another traditional dish eaten in Shanghai.

shanghai rice cakes with pork and cabbage

serves 4 / preparation time: 20 minutes / cooking time: 10 minutes

INGREDIENTS

Fresh Shanghai rice cakes	200 g
Chinese cabbage	200 g
Cooking oil	3 Tbsp
Garlic	2 cloves, peeled and minced
Lean pork	100 g, cut into strips
Water	150 ml
Sugar	to taste
Ground white pepper	to taste
Shao xing wine	1 Tbsp
Salt	to taste
Dark soy sauce	to taste
Light soy sauce	to taste

METHOD

- Cut rice cakes into serving sizes then blanch in hot water until soft and tender. Drain and soak in cold water to prevent rice cakes from sticking together.

- Cut Chinese cabbage into strips then blanch in hot water until 70% cooked. Drain and set aside.

- Heat oil in a wok and sauté garlic and pork until fragrant. Add water, sugar, pepper and wine and stir-fry. Cook until rice cakes are soft and flavours are absorbed.

- Lower heat and remove half portion of rice cakes. Add Chinese cabbage and salt to remaining rice cakes and stir-fry to prevent them from sticking to the wok. Dish out.

- Place other half of rice cakes in the same wok. Add dark and light soy sauce and stir-fry to colour rice cakes evenly. Remove and serve both rice cakes together immediately. You may serve this dish with some dark vinegar if desired.

chef's note: Shanghai rice cakes are usually cooked with either dark soy sauce or salt. For this recipe, I have combined the two cooking styles into one.

three coloured shanghai salted pork with rice

serves 1 / preparation time: 20 minutes / cooking time: 30 minutes

INGREDIENTS

Salted air-dried pork	80 g
Sichuan vegetable	1 small head
Baby white cabbage (*bai cai*)	6 stalks
Carrot	$1/3$
Shiitake mushrooms	2
Short grain rice	250 g
Cooking oil	2 Tbsp (optional)
Salt	to taste (optional)

METHOD

- Wash and cut air-dried pork, Sichuan vegetable, cabbage, carrot and mushrooms into small bits then put them aside separately.

- Wash rice and mix together with air-dried pork. Cook in a steamer or rice cooker.

- While waiting for the rice to cook, blanch Sichuan vegetable, cabbage, carrot and mushrooms separately in hot water. Drain and pat dry with absorbent paper.

- When rice is cooked, separate it into 3 equal portions while hot. Mix 1 portion with Sichuan vegetable and mushrooms, 1 with cabbage and 1 with carrot. Sprinkle in salt and oil if desired which mixing. (In the original Shanghai version, oil is used sparingly when cooking the vegetables and also when mixing with the rice.)

- Using a square mould, shape the rice. Place in a steamer to reheat for 5 minutes then transfer onto a serving plate. Remove mould and serve immediately.

chef's note: The original version of this dish consisted only of the minced baby white cabbage. I have added two more flavours to give the dish more depth in terms of taste, while at the same time making it more appealing in presentation. In some traditional restaurants, the chopped baby cabbage is mixed with the uncooked rice and salted pork then cooked together. I find that this overcooks the vegetable and causes it to lose its colour and vitamins. This is another reason for my version of the dish.

Air-dried salted pork can be substituted with Jinhua ham if preferred, but the ham needs to be blanched in hot water for some time to remove its excessive saltiness before using.

duo of roasted and steamed jasmine rice
with barbecued eel in superior broth

serves 4 / preparation time: 30 minutes / cooking time: 20 minutes

INGREDIENTS

Live white eel	1, about 500 g
Red capsicum (bell pepper)	1/2
Yellow capsicum (bell pepper)	1/2
Superior stock	600 ml (see pg 175)
Salt	a pinch
Sugar	to taste
Mei gui luo wine	2 tsp
Thai jasmine rice	150 g
Honey	1 Tbsp
Sesame seeds	1 Tbsp, roasted
Cooking oil	200 ml
Asparagus	1 spear, thinly sliced and blanched

seasoning

Light soy sauce	1 Tbsp
Hoisin sauce	1 Tbsp
Oyster sauce	2 tsp
Sesame oil	1 tsp
Dark soy sauce	1 tsp

METHOD

- Clean and debone live eel, keeping only the fillets. (Your seafood vendor can do this for you. A 500 g live eel should yield about 200 g of fillet after deboning.)

- Marinate eel fillets with combined seasoning. Set aside.

- Cut red and yellow capsicums into thin strips then soak in an ice bath to make them curl. Drain and reserve for garnish.

- Heat superior stock in a steamer or microwave oven. Season with salt, sugar and *mei gui luo* wine.

- Cook rice then spread half out on a plate and leave to dry using a fan or leave inside a warm oven (see *chef's note*).

- Preheat oven to 200°C. Place marinated eel onto a baking tray and bake for 15 minutes until cooked. Coat eel with a layer of honey while hot then sprinkle sesame seeds over. Cut into serving size pieces.

- While waiting for eel to be baked, heat oil in a wok and fry air-dried jasmine rice into rice crisps. They should be light golden brown in colour. Drain on absorbent paper.

- Press remaining half of steamed rice into a round mould and set in the centre of a serving plate. Remove mould and top with eel fillets. Place fried rice crisps and asparagus around rice. Garnish with capsicum curls. Pour boiling superior stock over just before serving.

chef's note: Roasted jasmine rice crisps can be prepared using leftover rice from the day before. They will keep for up to 2 weeks in an airtight container.

braised *ba bao* spicy sauce with shanghainese noodles

serves 2 / preparation time: 20 minutes / cooking time: 20 minutes

INGREDIENTS

Shanghainese noodles	200 g
Cooking oil	5 Tbsp
Garlic	2 cloves, peeled and minced
Potato flour	1 Tbsp, mixed with some water
Sesame oil	1 tsp

ba bao

Pressed bean curd	1 piece, cut into pieces the size of ginkgo nuts
Fresh ginkgo nuts	a handful, shelled
Chestnuts	5, peeled, soaked and cut into pieces the size of ginkgo nuts
Pig's stomach	50 g, cooked and cut into pieces the size of ginkgo nuts (see *chef's note*)
Edamame beans	a handful
Chicken leg	1
Dried prawns (shrimps)	a handful, soaked
Cashew nuts	a handful, roasted

seasoning

Hoisin sauce	1 Tbsp
Dark soy sauce	1 Tbsp
Sugar	to taste
Hot bean paste	1 Tbsp
Salt	to taste
Water	200 ml

METHOD

- Combine all seasoning ingredients in a bowl and mix well.
- Bring a pot of water to the boil and blanch *ba bao* ingredients separately. Drain and set aside.
- In another pot of water, blanch noodles until soft and drain well.
- Heat a wok with 2 Tbsp cooking oil and add half the combined seasoning. Bring to the boil then lower heat and add noodles. Leave to simmer until noodles are soft and flavours have been fully absorbed. Transfer to 2 serving dishes quickly. Cover to keep warm or keep warm in a steamer over low heat.
- Heat 1 Tbsp cooking oil in a clean wok and stir-fry blanched dried prawns until light golden brown in colour. Drain and discard oil.
- Clean wok and heat another 1 Tbsp cooking oil. Sauté garlic, blanched pig's stomach and chicken leg until fragrant. Add a little water if necessary. Set aside.
- Clean wok and heat remaining cooking oil. Add remaining half of combined seasoning and bring to the boil. Lower heat and add all *ba bao* ingredients. Leave to simmer until flavours are absorbed. Drain and ladle ingredients onto noodles.
- Thicken sauce with some potato flour solution then pour over noodles and serve immediately, sprinkled with some sesame oil.

chef's note The original version of this traditional Shanghai home-style dish called for ingredients like pig's stomach and chicken gizzards. But with the change in eating habits today, these ingredients can be substituted with other more common ingredients such as chicken, pork and duck to make up a total of eight different types of ingredients to honour the dish's Chinese name, *ba bao la jiang*, meaning "eight treasure spicy sauce".

braised eel strips and pickled mustard
with noodles in broth

serves 4 / preparation time: 20 minutes / cooking time: 10 minutes

INGREDIENTS

Pickled mustard	200 g, thinly shredded
Shanghai noodles	500 g
Basic stock	2 litres (see pg 175)
Salt	to taste
Sugar	to taste
Ground white pepper	a dash
Vegetable oil	150 ml
Garlic	2 cloves, peeled and minced
Fresh yellow eel strips	300 g
Bean sprouts	100 g
Dark soy sauce	2 tsp
Light soy sauce	to taste
Sesame oil	1 tsp
Potato flour	1 Tbsp, mixed with some water

METHOD

- Blanch shredded pickled mustard in hot water to remove excessive saltiness then rinse under running water for about 5 minutes. Drain and set aside.

- Bring a pot of water to the boil and blanch noodles until cooked. Divide into 4 serving bowls.

- Bring basic stock to the boil and season with salt, sugar and pepper.

- Heat 2 Tbsp oil in a wok and stir-fry garlic and eel strips until fragrant. Add 100 ml seasoned stock, bean sprouts and pickled mustard. Add dark and light soy sauces and sesame oil and mix well. Thicken sauce with some potato flour solution.

- Top noodles with fried eel strips and pour boiling stock over. Serve immediately. Garnish as desired.

Dim Sum

For most Chinese, dim sum is enjoyed at breakfast time.
But the Shanghainese prefer to have their dim sum at the end
of the meal, just before dessert, and often with noodles or rice.

At Shanghai's dim sum pinnacle sits the enthralling *xiao long bao*, which when made by the most accomplished dim sum chef, should boast 18 to 24 neat little pleats. Equally charming is *luo bo si su bing* (white radish pastry) which is so delicate that it cannot withstand the pressure of a pair of chopsticks or a fork. The best way to enjoy this light and fluffy pastry is to carefully place the whole thing in your mouth with your fingers! *Ba bao tian fan* (eight treasure sweet rice) is often mistaken for a dessert, but it is traditionally considered a dim sum another traditional favorite using eight varieties of sugar cured dried fruits and raisins, arranged neatly on top of sweet glutinous rice. And how can we miss out *cong you bing* (onion pancakes)? Its rich flavours and robust fragrance of scallions attracts a crowd at dawn each day on the many street corners in town.

shanghai *xiao long bao* pork dumplings

makes 35 / preparation time: 40 minutes / cooking time: 10 minutes

INGREDIENTS

Pork belly (40% fat, 60% lean meat)	600 g, minced and chilled
Egg	1
Potato flour	2 tsp
Salt	to taste
Water chestnuts	75 g, peeled and finely chopped
Spring onions (scallions)	2, finely chopped
Coriander (cilantro) leaves	75 g, finely chopped
Young ginger	150 g, peeled, half shredded and half finely chopped
Pork skin jelly	300 g (see *chef's note*)
Plain (all-purpose) flour	225 g
High-gluten flour	75 g
Wo sun shoot	1, peeled
Hon shimeji mushrooms	100 g
Flying fish roe	50 g
Black vinegar	

seasoning

Sugar	to taste
Ground white pepper	a dash
Sesame oil	4 tsp
Dark soy sauce	2 tsp

METHOD

- Place chilled minced meat in a large mixing bowl and add egg, potato flour and salt. Mix in one direction until mixture starts to bind together. Add seasoning, water chestnuts, spring onions, coriander and chopped ginger and continue to mix in the same direction until well mixed. Add pork skin jelly and mix well. Chill filling until ready to use.

- Prepare dumpling skin. Combine high-gluten and plain flours. Take a quarter of the combined flour and pour in enough boiling water to get a smooth dough. Add enough tap water to the remaining flour to get another smooth dough. Combine both mixtures and knead into a smooth dough.

- Divide dumpling skin dough into 35 pieces and roll each one out into a thin circle. Spoon some filling onto each skin and pleat edges to seal.

- Using only the tender part of *wo sun* shoot, cut it into thin 4-cm strips.

- Insert a mushroom and a strip of *wo sun* shoot into the top of every dumpling and steam over high heat for 5–6 minutes until cooked.

- Garnish dumplings with flying fish roe and serve with shredded ginger and black vinegar.

chef's note: Pork skin jelly is the secret to the juicy Shanghai *xiao long bao* dumplings. Clean 500 g pork skin by using a small pincer to remove any visible hairs on it. Blanch in a pot of hot water for about 2 minutes to remove any impurities then allow to cool before cutting into 10-cm squares. Heat some oil in a wok and stir-fry a knob of ginger and some spring onions until fragrant. Add 900 ml water, 200 ml *shao xing* wine and pork skin squares. Bring to the boil then transfer to a large heatproof (flameproof) bowl and steam for about 2 hours. Discard ginger and spring onions then blend (process) mixture. Pass blended mixture through a sieve and retain the liquid. Season to taste with salt and allow liquid to cool. It will set into a jelly. Cover and keep refrigerated. Pork skin jelly will keep in the refrigerator for a few weeks. Use a clean spoon to scoop the jelly when needed and cover properly after use.

pan-fried juicy *sheng jian* meat dumpling

makes 28 / preparation time: 40 minutes / cooking time: 10 minutes

INGREDIENTS

White sesame seeds	1 Tbsp
Black vinegar	

filling

Pork belly	500 g, finely minced and chilled
Potato flour	2 tsp
Salt	to taste
Spring onions (scallions)	2, minced
Dried Chinese mushrooms	2, soaked to soften and cut into small cubes
Ginger	5-cm knob, peeled, half shredded and half minced
Pork skin jelly	250 g, (see *chef's note*, pg 153)

dumpling skin

Instant dried yeast	$^1/_4$ tsp
Baking soda	$^1/_4$ tsp
Water	150 ml
High-gluten flour	240 g

seasoning

Sugar	to taste
Ground white pepper	a dash
Sesame oil	4 tsp
Light soy sauce	2 tsp
Dark soy sauce	2 tsp

METHOD

- Prepare filling. Place chilled minced meat into a large mixing bowl and add potato flour and salt. Mix in one direction until mixture starts to bind together. Add seasoning ingredients, spring onions, mushrooms and minced ginger and continue mixing in the same direction until well mixed. Add pork skin jelly and mix well. Refrigerate until ready to use.

- Prepare dumpling skin. Dissolve yeast and baking soda in water. Add to flour and knead into a smooth dough. Wrap dough with plastic wrap and leave to rest for about 20 minutes before use.

- Divide dumpling skin dough into 28 pieces, each about 20 g. Roll each piece out into a thin circle. Spoon some filling onto each piece and pleat edges to seal.

- Heat a non-stick pan and use an oiled cloth to grease it lightly. Place dumplings in pan and pour hot water in. The water should come up to 0.5-cm the height of the pan. Cover and bring to the boil.

- When water boils, uncover pan and sprinkle some sesame seeds over dumplings. Replace cover and immediately lower heat to simmer for 7–8 minutes until water evaporates and bottom of dumplings are golden brown and dumplings are cooked. Serve immediately with ginger sheds and black vinegar.

siew mai in three flavours with fresh bamboo shoots

makes 30 / preparation time: 1 hour / cooking time: 10 minutes

INGREDIENTS

Lean pork	300 g, cut into 0.8-cm cubes and chilled
Egg	1
Potato flour	$^1/_2$ Tbsp
Salt	to taste
Tiger prawns (shrimp) meat	300 g, deveined, lightly chopped and chilled
Dried Chinese mushrooms	3, soaked to soften and minced
Pork fat	75 g, finely minced
High-gluten flour	180 g
Plain (all-purpose) flour	180 g
Carrot juice	100 ml (see *chef's note*)
Bird's eye chillies	2, minced
Spinach juice	100 ml (see *chef's note*)
Winter bamboo shoots	3, peeled
Siew mai skin	10 sheets

seasoning

Sugar	to taste
Ground white pepper	a dash
Sesame oil	2 tsp
Shallot oil	3 Tbsp (see pg 43)

METHOD

- Place chilled lean pork into a large mixing bowl and add egg, potato flour and salt to taste. Mix in one direction until mixture starts to bind together. Add prawns, seasoning, mushrooms and pork fat and continue mixing in the same direction until well mixed. Refrigerate filling until ready to use.

- Prepare dumpling skin. Combine high-gluten and plain flours together then divide into 2 equal portions. Further divide 1 portion into 4 equal parts for carrot-chilli skin.

- For carrot-chilli skin, heat carrot juice and add some to 1 part of flour. Mix well. Add remaining carrot juice to remaining 3 parts of flour and combine with minced chillies. Combine both flour mixtures and knead into a smooth dough.

- For spinach skin, heat spinach juice and add to remaining portion of flour. Mix well and knead into a smooth dough.

- Using a domestic pasta-making machine, roll the two coloured doughs out separately until they are thin enough. Use a 6-cm round pastry cutter to cut out 10 circles from dough sheets. Sprinkle some plain flour over pastry circles to prevent sticking. Cover with a cloth so dough does not dry up.

- Use only the tender top part of bamboo shoots and cut into thin 4-cm strips. Blanch in hot water for 5 minutes until cooked. Drain.

- Spoon some chilled filling onto a *siew mai* skin and bring the edges up to make a *siew mai*. The filling should be exposed at the top. Repeat to make 30 *siew mai* with *siew mai* skin, carrot-chilli skin and spinach skin. Top each *siew mai* with some bamboo shoots strips.

- Steam *siew mai* over boiling water over high heat for 5–6 minutes until cooked. Serve immediately.

chef's note: The quantity of water required to make the dumpling dough varies, depending on the quality and age of the flours. As a general rule, use 1 part liquid to 2 parts flour. The dough should be soft enough to be rolled out and not crack (too dry) or stick to your fingers (too moist).

To extract carrot or spinach juice, blend (process) the vegetable with some water then pass the puree through a sieve. Discard the pulp and use the juice.

spring onion and pork floss pancakes

serves 6 / preparation time: 40 minutes / cooking time: 10 minutes

INGREDIENTS

Spring onions (scallions)	300 g, cut into 0.3-cm pieces
Pork fat	300 g, cut into 0.3-cm pieces
Pork floss	75 g
High-gluten flour	150 g
Plain (all-purpose) flour	150 g
Vegetable shortening	150 g
Sugar	1 tsp
Water	150 ml
Cooking oil	500 ml

seasoning

Salt	to taste
Sugar	to taste
Sesame oil	1 Tbsp
Ground white pepper	a dash

METHOD

- Combine spring onions and pork fat in a mixing bowl and add seasoning to taste. Add pork floss and lightly chill mixture before use.

- Combine high-gluten and plain flours, vegetable shortening, sugar and about 150 ml water and knead into a dough. Let dough rest for about 15 minutes then divide into 20 equal portions. Roll each portion out into a flat rectangular skin. Spoon some filling onto each skin and roll up. Use some water to seal the edges and ends.

- Cover a heatproof (flameproof) plate with plastic wrap and arrange dumplings evenly on it. Steam over boiling water for 20–30 seconds until outer layer of dumplings are heated. Remove from steamer and allow to cool. (This process will prevent the dumpling skin from cracking and give the dumplings a nicer colour as the sugar in the dumpling skin melts completely.)

- Heat oil in a wok over medium heat. Deep-fry dumplings in batches until cooked and light golden brown in colour. Drain on absorbent paper. Serve immediately.

shanghai style fluffy radish dumplings

makes 35 / preparation time: 5 hours / cooking time: 10 minutes

INGREDIENTS

oil-based dough

Plain (all-purpose) flour	600 g
Vegetable shortening	250 g
Butter	75 g

water-based dough

Plain (all-purpose) flour	480 g
Bread flour	150 g
Vegetable shortening	180 g
Sugar	75 g
Water	300 ml

filling

White radish	600 g, peeled and cut into 8 x 0.3-cm strips
Jinhua ham	50 g, minced
Sugar	15 g
Salt	to taste
Potato flour	1 Tbsp, mixed with some water

METHOD

- Combine oil-based dough ingredients and mix thoroughly using a pastry scraper to get a soft dough. Spread dough out onto a tray and store in the freezer for about 30 minutes.
- Combine water-based dough ingredients and knead into a smooth dough. (This can be done by hand with a pastry scarpper or with an electric cake mixer.)
- Place water-based dough on top of oil-based dough and roll out. Place combined dough to chill at 0°–5°C for 4 hours before use.
- Roll chilled dough out into a large rectangular shape. Fold it into 3 then roll out and fold into 3 again to create a layered pastry dough skin. Wrap with plastic wrap so dough does not dry up. Refrigerate until ready to use.
- Prepare filling. Blanch radish strips in hot water for 1 minute then drain well. Heat 50 ml water in a pan and add minced ham, sugar and salt to taste. Thicken mixture with potato flour solution then transfer to a serving plate to cool. (Cooling the filling will make it easier to handle when folding the dumplings.)
- Divide dough skin into 35 pieces, each about 15 g. Roll out into thin skins. Spoon some filling onto each skin and fold into an oblong shape. Make 35 dumplings in total.
- Heat oil to medium heat (160°–180°C) and deep-fry dumplings until light golden brown in colour. Drain well and serve immediately.

Desserts

Finding exciting, visually attractive desserts has always
been a challenge in Chinese cuisine.
Even the classics have become a little stale and boring.

Most traditional offerings are straightforward, offering painfully little contrast in texture, taste or presentation. Nonetheless, enjoying Shanghainese desserts like jiu niang yuan zi (glutinous rice flour pearls in rice wine brine) and dou sha guo bing (red bean pancake) have become a time honoured tradition. But at Whampoa Club we've decided to push the envelope and modernise our desserts while retaining their Chinese essence. Having been trained in classical desserts, we took all-familiar items like mango pudding, warm sesame soup and walnut paste to be our basic building blocks and introduced European pastry traditions into the Chinese dessert oeuvre. As a result, we're among the first in Shanghai to introduce desserts that, at their cores, remain Chinese, yet they've won over diners with novel flavour pairings and scintillating contrasts—hot sesame soup topped with ginger-scented egg-white and milk custard, served with a melt-in-your-mouth puff pastry stuffed with a red date paste; warm chocolate cake filled with bananas and almonds served with cold sago honey dew soup.

chinese *pi pa gao* ice cream

serves 4 / preparation time: 10 minutes / cooking time: 20 minutes

INGREDIENTS

ice cream

Full cream milk	200 ml
Whipped cream	200 g
Sugar	40 g
Egg yolks	5, beaten, or use pasteurised liquid eggs
Nian chi an pi pa gao	40 ml

almond crisps

Almonds flakes	50 g, roasted
Water	60 ml
Sugar	230 g
Glucose	15 ml

METHOD

- Prepare ice cream. Combine milk and whipped cream in a pot and bring to the boil. Remove from heat and stir in sugar. Keep stirring until sugar dissolves completely. Add egg yolks and continue stirring all the time. Add *pi pa gao* and stir until dissolved.

- Pour into an ice cream machine and blend until a smooth ice cream is formed. Freeze until ready to use.

- Prepare almond crisps. Spread a thin layer of roasted almond flakes onto a pastry flexi pad, leaving a margin around the sides.

- Heat water and sugar in a copper or stainless steel pan over low heat. Stir until sugar is completely dissolved. Wash down the sides of the pan with water using a brush dedicated for sugar boiling.

- Bring mixture to a rolling boil then add glucose and lower heat immediately. Do not stir once the sugar starts boiling. Brush down the sides of the pan with water as needed until the temperature of the sugar reaches 138°C. Leave to boil until mixture has caramelised into a golden brown colour.

- Quickly pour sugar over roasted almond flakes, spreading it out as thinly as possible. Allow to cool before breaking into desired shapes.

- Scoop ice cream into balls and place into serving bowls. Here, I have used hand-pulled coloured sugar cups. Garnish with almond crisps and serve immediately.

mini version of shanghai's eight treasure rice

serves 2 / preparation time: 15 minutes / cooking time: 45 minutes

INGREDIENTS

Glutinous rice	60 g, soaked for 2 hours then drained
Black glutinous rice	120 g, soaked for 2 hours then drained
Vegetable shortening	50 g
Sugar	to taste
Cooked lotus seeds	12 (see *chef's note*)
Raisins	50 g
Red bean paste	50 g
Coconut cream	4 Tbsp
Preserved orange peel	20 g, julienned

METHOD

- Combine glutinous rice and mix evenly.
- Line a bamboo steamer with muslin cloth and spread glutinous rice out on it. Steam for 30 minutes until cooked.
- Combine hot glutinous rice with vegetable shortening, sugar and cooked lotus seeds. Mix until sugar is completely melted.
- Line several small moulds with plastic wrap. Place some raisins into the base of moulds, leaving a hole in the centre. Fill with some red bean paste and top with a layer of glutinous rice.
- Place moulds in a steamer to re-heat before serving. Remove rice from moulds and arrange on serving dishes. Top with coconut cream and preserved orange peel before serving.

chef's note: Canned lotus seeds are already cooked, so they can be used straight from the can.

If using fresh lotus seeds, use a toothpick to remove the bitter centre part from the seeds then soak the seeds in a light sugar syrup (about 30 g sugar to 100 ml water) and steam for about 30 minutes until soft to the bite.

If using dried lotus seeds, soak them in water for 30 minutes until softened then follow the same preparation method as fresh lotus seeds.

snow frog and aloe vera yoghurt mousse

serves 6 / preparation time: 30 minutes / cooking time: 30 minutes

INGREDIENTS

sponge cake

Plain (all-purpose) flour	110 g, sifted
Corn flour (cornstarch)	110 g, sifted
Eggs	12
Sugar	200 g

mousse

Gelatin	14 sheets, about 28 g
Egg whites	3
Sugar	100 g
Water	50 ml
Yoghurt	250 ml
Milk	250 ml
Ready-to-eat aloe vera	200 g
Cooked snow frog glands (*hasima*)	100 g (see *chef's note*)

garnish

Raspberries	100 g
Mint leaves	
Custard cream	100 ml (see *chef's note*)
Chocolate sticks	
Pulled sugar	

METHOD

- Prepare sponge cake. Combine flours and set aside. Beat eggs and sugar with a whisk or electric cake mixer until mixture is light and fluffy and holds its own shape. Fold flour in a little at a time.

- Preheat oven to 170°C. Line a shallow baking tray with greaseproof paper and pour sponge cake mixture over. Bake for about 10 minutes until light golden brown in colour. (Insert a bamboo skewer into the centre of the cake to test for doneness. If the cake is cooked, the skewer will come out clean. If not, bake for a little while longer.)

- Prepare mousse. Soak gelatin sheets in cold water until softened. Drain then place in a pot. Fill with enough water to cover gelatin sheets then bring to the boil over low heat and stir until completely dissolved. Set aside.

- Beat egg whites and a third of the sugar with a whisk or electric cake mixer until mixture is fluffy and holds its own shape.

- Add remaining sugar to water and bring to the boil stirring to dissolve sugar. Pour sugar syrup into beaten egg whites and stir continuously until cooled. Add yoghurt, milk, gelatin solution, aloe vera and snow frog glands.

- Place sponge cake into a cake tin and top with a thick layer of aloe vera mousse. Chill well before removing from tin and cutting. Garnish with raspberries, mint leaves, custard cream, chocolate sticks and pulled sugar or as desired.

chef's note: Prepare custard cream by combining 100 ml cream, 1 tsp custard powder and 15 g sugar. Chill well before use.

To prepare snow frog glands, first use a pincer to pick out as much of the black dots and skin-like membrane. Soak in warm water until glands expand to 30 times its original weight. Drain and place in a heatproof (flameproof) bowl together with some lightly smashed ginger. Add enough water to cover glands and steam for about 15 minutes. Drain and soak glands in cold water. Steam to reheat when ready to use.

photograph on pg 169

chilled sorbet of osmanthus blossom wine

serves 4 / preparation time: 5 minutes / cooking time: 5 hours

INGREDIENTS

Sugar	80 g
Hot water	50 ml
Ice cubes	400 g
Osmanthus blossom wine (*gui hua chen jiu*)	160 ml
Fresh or dried Osmanthus blossoms	10 g

METHOD

- Combine sugar and hot water to melt sugar. Place over low heat if necessary until sugar is completely dissolved. Leave to cool.
- Crush ice cubes and mix with wine. Stir in cooled sugar syrup according to taste.
- Add fresh or dried Osmanthus blossoms and mix well. Pour into a shallow dish and spread it out evenly.
- Place in the freezer until hardened. When ready to serve, use a stainless steel spoon to shave the ice out. Spoon into small cups and serve immediately.

shanghai glutinous pearls in rice wine brine

serves 4 / preparation time: 30 minutes / cooking time: 10 minutes

INGREDIENTS

Red capsicum (bell pepper)	1
Spinach leaves	50 g
Carrot	50 g, chopped
Sugar	30 g
Glutinous rice flour	150 g
Wheat starch flour	30 g
Vegetable shortening	2 tsp

rice wine brine

Water	400 ml
Sugar	90 g
Sweet rice wine brine	50 g

METHOD

- Make a few cuts on the skin of capsicum and bake in a pre-heated oven at 180°C for about 5 minutes. Remove from oven, peel away skin and discard, keeping only the flesh. Cut capsicum into smaller pieces.

- Using an electric blender (processor), blend capsicum, spinach and carrot separately, adding a little water each time. Pass purees separately through a sieve, discarding the pulp and keeping only the juices. Stir 10 g sugar into each juice.

- Combine glutinous rice flour and wheat starch flour. Divide into 4 equal portions. Mix the 3 juices separately into 3 portions of flour and knead until smooth. Add the juices gradually so the right consistency of dough is achieved. Use some vegetable shortening as necessary. Mix the remaining portion of flour with some water and vegetable shortening to form a white-coloured dough.

- Divide each colour of dough into small 1-cm pieces then roll into balls.

- Bring a pot of water to the boil and cook dough balls until they float to the surface of the water. Drain and keep dough balls soaked in water until ready to serve. This will prevent them from clumping together.

- Prepare rice wine brine. Bring water to the boil and stir in sugar and sweet rice wine brine. Drain dough balls and add to brine. Return to the boil and serve immediately.

Basic Recipes

superior stock

INGREDIENTS

Stewing hen	1, about 750 g
Lean pork	3 kg
Jinhua ham	600 g
Water	7.5 litres

METHOD

- Blanch stewing hen, pork and ham in hot water to remove any impurities.
- Bring water to the boil and place blanched ingredients in. Lower heat and simmer for about 6 hours to get about 3 litres stock after straining. Keep stewing hen, pork and ham for making basic stock if desired.

basic stock

INGREDIENTS

Stewing hen	1, about 300 g
Pork bones	1 kg (see *chef's note*)
Water	7.5 litres

METHOD

- Blanch chicken and pork bones in hot water to remove any impurities.
- Bring water to the boil and place blanched ingredients in. (Add any additional meat from making superior stock.) Lower heat and simmer for about 6 hours to get about 3 litres stock after straining.

chef's note: If only preparing basic stock without first making superior stock, increase the amount of pork bones to 2 kg.

Glossary

Bai Ye **Bean Curd Skin**
This is a specialty of Shanghai. It is bean curd skin that has been processed with lye water to give it a crunchy texture. *Bai ye* bean curd adds a pleasant, unique flavour to soups.

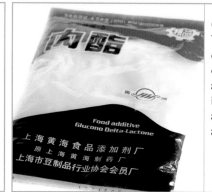

Glucono Delta Lactone (GDL)
This is a powdered food additive commonly used in the production of bean curd. It is white in colour and is practically odourless. It helps in the coagulation of the soy milk and gives the resulting bean curd a very fine texture.

Brown Wheat Gluten (*Kao Fu*)
This is another specialty of Shanghai. It is made of air-dried wheat flour and has a unique texture and natural flavour that makes it hard to substitute. The closest alternative if brown wheat gluten is not available is a vegetarian dough known as *mian jin*.

Truffles
Truffles are a kind of mushroom and are considered a delicacy. Chinese truffles resemble French black truffles visually, but they are not as aromatic or intense in flavour.

Chinese Vinegar
China-produced vinegars are made by fermenting rice or glutinous rice with cereals, spices and sugar. The quality varies greatly among brands.

Kou Shan Si **Mould**
This mould looks like an ordinary Chinese teacup, but it has a hole at the base to facilitate removing the moulded ingredients and plating them nicely.

Shanghai Rice Cakes

Made from glutinous rice flour, these rice cakes are soft and chewy and can be used in both sweet and savoury preparations. It is commonly eaten during the Chinese New Year season, since in Chinese, it is known as "*nian gao*", meaning to achieve more and more with each passing year.

Monkey Head Mushrooms

These mushrooms are also known as bear's head or lion's mane mushrooms. They have a strong woody flavour and are favoured for their nutritional value and their ability to boost a person's immunity.

Sea Cucumber, dried and soaked

Soaked sea cucumber is available in many Chinese dried seafood specialty shops. Good quality sea cucumber will turn soft but will not melt and break into pieces when cooked over slow heat. Soaking of dried sea cucumber is a complicated process that requires 4–5 days' work. It involves removing the hard outer crust of the sea cucumber by roasting over flames and then soaking it in hot water repeatedly to rehydrate it.

Green Pea Starch Strips

This dried noodle is made from green bean flour. In its dried form, it is clear. It becomes white when boiled or reconstituted in water. These noodles have no flavour on its own, so it lends itself very well to many ingredients, taking on the flavour of the ingredients it is cooked with.

Dried Prawn Roe

This is made from the roe of prawns harvested from the sea or from freshwater. The roe is removed from the prawns then dried to create this rich and pungent ingredient. It is commonly used in cooking with bean curd, eggs, meats, soups, or just sprinkled over dishes for their wonderful flavour.

Osmanthus Blossoms (*Gui Hua*), sweet and salted

These tiny yellow flowers are from a Chinese evergreen. They have a fresh floral scent and are used in flavouring teas and desserts, and making perfumes. They are commonly available in Chinese herbal stores or provision shops. If well-kept and refrigerated, these blossoms can keep indefinitely.

Red Yeast Powder (*Hong Qu*)

This edible red coloured powder is made from rice and red yeast through fermentation. It is commonly used in traditional Shanghainese cooking to enhance the colour and flavour of food.

 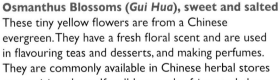 

Glossary

Wa Wa Cabbage

Wa wa cabbage actually translates to baby cabbage. It looks like Chinese cabbage and has a similar oblong shape and closely-packed pale green leaves with wide stems, but it is only about 15-cm long. *Wa wa* cabbage can be cooked whole without first separating the leaves.

Ji Cai

This vegetable used to grow wild and was only available during the cold season in Shanghai. Today however, it is cultivated and is commonly available all year round. *Ji cai* is usually boiled and used in salads such as Shanghai's cold dish selection.

Stem Lettuce (Wo Sun)

This vegetable is cultivated in northen China and is available all year round. The stems and leaves are used separately but the choicest part of the vegetable is the stem. The stem is usually simply blanched or stir-fried in dishes and remains crunchy even after cooking.

Weights and Measures

Quantities for this book are given in Metric and American (spoon and cup) measures. Standard spoon and cup measurements used are: I teaspoon = 5 ml, I tablespoon = 15 ml, I cup = 250 ml. All measures are level unless otherwise stated.

LIQUID AND VOLUME MEASURES

Metric	Imperial	American
5 ml	$^1/_6$ fl oz	I teaspoon
10 ml	$^1/_3$ fl oz	I dessertspoon
15 ml	$^1/_2$ fl oz	I tablespoon
60 ml	2 fl oz	$^1/_4$ cup (4 tablespoons)
85 ml	$2^1/_2$ fl oz	$^1/_3$ cup
90 ml	3 fl oz	$^3/_8$ cup (6 tablespoons)
125 ml	4 fl oz	$^1/_2$ cup
180 ml	6 fl oz	$^3/_4$ cup
250 ml	8 fl oz	I cup
300 ml	10 fl oz ($^1/_2$ pint)	$1^1/_4$ cups
375 ml	12 fl oz	$1^1/_2$ cups
435 ml	14 fl oz	$1^3/_4$ cups
500 ml	16 fl oz	2 cups
625 ml	20 fl oz (I pint)	$2^1/_2$ cups
750 ml	24 fl oz ($1^1/_5$ pints)	3 cups
I litre	32 fl oz ($1^3/_5$ pints)	4 cups
1.25 litres	40 fl oz (2 pints)	5 cups
1.5 litres	48 fl oz ($2^2/_5$ pints)	6 cups
2.5 litres	80 fl oz (4 pints)	10 cups

DRY MEASURES

Metric	Imperial
30 grams	I ounce
45 grams	$1^1/_2$ ounces
55 grams	2 ounces
70 grams	$2^1/_2$ ounces
85 grams	3 ounces
100 grams	$3^1/_2$ ounces
110 grams	4 ounces
125 grams	$4^1/_2$ ounces
140 grams	5 ounces
280 grams	10 ounces
450 grams	16 ounces (I pound)
500 grams	I pound, $1^1/_2$ ounces
700 grams	$1^1/_2$ pounds
800 grams	$1^3/_4$ pounds
I kilogram	2 pounds, 3 ounces
1.5 kilograms	3 pounds, $4^1/_2$ ounces
2 kilograms	4 pounds, 6 ounces

LENGTH

Metric	Imperial
0.5 cm	$^1/_4$ inch
I cm	$^1/_2$ inch
1.5 cm	$^3/_4$ inch
2.5 cm	I inch

OVEN TEMPERATURE

	°C	°F	Gas Regulo
Very slow	120	250	I
Slow	150	300	2
Moderately slow	160	325	3
Moderate	180	350	4
Moderately hot	190/200	370/400	5/6
Hot	210/220	410/440	6/7
Very hot	230	450	8
Super hot	250/290	475/550	9/10

ABBREVIATION

tsp	teaspoon
tbsp	tablespoon
g	gram
kg	kilogram
ml	millilitre

Jereme and his team at Whampoa Club, Shanghai.

Editor : Lydia Leong
Designer : Lynn Chin Nyuk Ling
Photographer : Edmond Ho
Writer : Tan Su Lyn

The publisher wishes to thank **Asianera** and **Simplylife** for the loan and use of their tableware.

© **2005 Marshall Cavendish International (Asia) Private Limited**
Published by Marshall Cavendish Cuisine
An imprint of Marshall Cavendish International (Asia) Private Limited
A member of Times Publishing Limited
Times Centre, 1 New Industrial Road, Singapore 536196
Tel: (65) 6213 9300 Fax: (65) 6285 4871
E-mail: te@sg.marshallcavendish.com
Online Bookstore: www.marshallcavendish.com/genref

Malaysian Office:
Marshall Cavendish (Malaysia) Sdn Bhd (3024-D)
(General & Reference Publishing)
(Formerly known as Federal Publications Sdn Berhad)
Times Subang, Lot 46, Persiaran Teknologi Subang
Subang Hi-Tech Industrial Park
Batu Tiga, 40000 Shah Alam
Selangor Darul Ehsan, Malaysia
Tel: (603) 5635 2191, 5628 6888 Fax: (603) 5635 2706
E-mail: cchong@my.marshallcavendish.com

National Library Board Singapore Cataloguing in Publication Data

Leung, Jereme, 1971-
New Shanghai cuisine : bridging the old and the new / Jereme Leung.
– Singapore :
Marshall Cavendish Cuisine, c2005.
p. cm.
Includes index.
ISBN : 981-232-698-7

1. Cookery, Chinese. 2. Cookery – China – Shanghai. I. Title.

TX724.5.C5
641.5951132 -- dc21   SLS2005024417

Printed in Singapore by Tien Wah Press (Pte) Ltd